LEVEL 5 Supplemental
ANSWER BOOK

By Glory St. Germain ARCT RMT MYCC UMTC &
Shelagh McKibbon-U'Ren RMT UMTC

The LEVEL 5 Supplemental Workbook is designed to be completed
after the Basic Rudiments and LEVEL 4 Supplemental Workbook.

GSG MUSIC
Enriching Lives Through Music Education

ISBN: 978-1-927641-56-9

The Ultimate Music Theory™ Program

The Ultimate Music Theory™ Program lays the foundation of music theory education.

The focus of the Ultimate Music Theory Program is to simplify complex concepts and show the relativity of these concepts with practical application. This program is designed to help teachers and students discover the excitement and benefits of a sound music theory education.

The Ultimate Music Theory Program is based on a proven approach to the study of music theory that follows the *"must have"* Learning Principles to develop effective learning for all learning styles.

The Ultimate Music Theory™ Program and Supplemental Workbooks help students prepare for nationally recognized theory examinations including the Royal Conservatory of Music.

GSG MUSIC

Library and Archives Canada Cataloguing in Publication
UMT Supplemental Series / Glory St. Germain and Shelagh McKibbon-U'Ren

Gloryland Publishing - UMT Supplemental Workbook and Answer Book Series:

GP-SPL	ISBN: 978-1-927641-41-5	UMT Supplemental Prep Level
GP-SL1	ISBN: 978-1-927641-42-2	UMT Supplemental Level 1
GP-SL2	ISBN: 978-1-927641-43-9	UMT Supplemental Level 2
GP-SL3	ISBN: 978-1-927641-44-6	UMT Supplemental Level 3
GP-SL4	ISBN: 978-1-927641-45-3	UMT Supplemental Level 4
GP-SL5	ISBN: 978-1-927641-46-0	UMT Supplemental Level 5
GP-SL6	ISBN: 978-1-927641-47-7	UMT Supplemental Level 6
GP-SL7	ISBN: 978-1-927641-48-4	UMT Supplemental Level 7
GP-SL8	ISBN: 978-1-927641-49-1	UMT Supplemental Level 8
GP-SCL	ISBN: 978-1-927641-50-7	UMT Supplemental Complete Level
GP-SPLA	ISBN: 978-1-927641-51-4	UMT Supplemental Prep Level Answer Book
GP-SL1A	ISBN: 978-1-927641-52-1	UMT Supplemental Level 1 Answer Book
GP-SL2A	ISBN: 978-1-927641-53-8	UMT Supplemental Level 2 Answer Book
GP-SL3A	ISBN: 978-1-927641-54-5	UMT Supplemental Level 3 Answer Book
GP-SL4A	ISBN: 978-1-927641-55-2	UMT Supplemental Level 4 Answer Book
GP-SL5A	ISBN: 978-1-927641-56-9	UMT Supplemental Level 5 Answer Book
GP-SL6A	ISBN: 978-1-927641-57-6	UMT Supplemental Level 6 Answer Book
GP-SL7A	ISBN: 978-1-927641-58-3	UMT Supplemental Level 7 Answer Book
GP-SL8A	ISBN: 978-1-927641-59-0	UMT Supplemental Level 8 Answer Book
GP-SCLA	ISBN: 978-1-927641-60-6	UMT Supplemental Complete Level Answer Book

Respect Copyright - Copyright 2017 Gloryland Publishing

All rights reserved. No part of this publication may be reproduced or transmitted in any form or by any means, electronic or mechanical, including photocopying, recording, or any information storage and retrieval system, without permission in writing from the author/publisher.

* Resources - An annotated list is available at UltimateMusicTheory.com under Free Resources.

Ultimate Music Theory
LEVEL 5 Supplemental
Table of Contents

Ultimate Music Theory	The Story of UMT... Meet So-La & Ti-Do	4
Comparison Chart	Level 5	6
Dotted Note/Rest Values	Stem Direction and Notes with Beams	8
Two-Part Music	Stems, Beams and Rest Placement	12
Compound Time	Introduction to 6/8 Time & Compound Basic Beat	14
Rests in 6/8 Time	Comparing 3/4 (Simple)Time and 6/8 (Compound)Time	16
Rhythm and Meter	Adding Bar Lines and Adding Rests	18
Circle of Fifths	Major and Relative Minor Keys (4 sharps and 4 flats)	20
Minor Scales	Writing using a Key Signature and using Accidentals	22
Technical Degrees	Parallel Keys and Relative Keys	24
Identifying Intervals	Monophonic, Homophonic and Polyphonic Texture	26
Parallel and Contrary	Chromatic & Diatonic Steps and Enharmonic Equivalents	30
Parallel Triads	Primary Triads and Chord Symbols	32
Triad Positions	Root Position, First and Second Inversions	34
Chord Symbols	Symbol Identification, Solid and Broken Triads	36
Writing Triads	Root/Quality Chord Symbols & Functional Chord Symbols	40
Dominant 7th Chords	Major Keys & Minor Keys and Accidental Placement	42
Broken Triads/Chords	Close Position Chords & Game - Feed the Fish	46
Musical Terms & Signs	Term Review - Suffixes - *etto* and *issimo*	50
Transposing	Up or Down One Octave & Same Pitch in the Alternate Clef	52
Composing	Question & Answer Parallel Period	54
Analysis of Melodies	Melody & Chords, Melodic Phrases (a, a1, b)	58
Melody Writing	Imagine, Compose, Explore & Sight Reading - Slippery Snake	62
Music History Voices	Genre, Performing Forces, Relationship between Music & Text	64
G. F. Handel	Analysis of Hallelujah Chorus from Messiah	66
W. A. Mozart	Analysis of Queen of the Night from The Magic Flute	68
H. Arlen	Analysis of Over the Rainbow from The Wizard of Oz	70
Music History Review	Composers, Compositions, Genre, Performing Forces, etc.	72
Theory Exam	Level 5	73
Certificate	Completion of Level 5	80

Score: 60 - 69 Pass; **70 - 79** Honors; **80 - 89** First Class Honors; **90 - 100** First Class Honors with Distinction

Ultimate Music Theory: *The Way to Score Success!*

Workbooks, Exams, Answers, Online Courses, App & More!

A Proven Step-by-Step System to Learn Theory Faster - from Beginner to Advanced.

Innovative techniques designed to develop a complete understanding of music theory, to enhance sight reading, ear training, creativity, composition and musical expression.

All UMT Series have matching Answer Books!

The UMT Rudiments Series - Beginner A, Beginner B, Beginner C, Prep 1, Prep 2, Basic, Intermediate, Advanced & Complete (All-In-One)

♪ 12 Lessons, Review Tests, and a Final Exam to develop confidence
♪ Music Theory Guide & Chart for fast and easy reference of theory concepts
♪ 80 Flashcards for fun drills to dramatically increase retention & comprehension

Rudiments Exam Series - Preparatory, Basic, Intermediate & Advanced

♪ 8 Exams plus UMT Tips on How to Score 100% on Theory Exams

Each Rudiments Workbook correlates to a Supplemental Workbook.

The UMT Supplemental Series - Prep Level, Level 1, Level 2, Level 3, Level 4, Level 5, Level 6, Level 7, Level 8 & Complete (All-In-One) Level

♪ Form & Analysis and Music History - Composers, Eras & Musical Styles
♪ Melody Writing using ICE - Imagine, Compose & Explore
♪ 12 Lessons, Review Tests, Final Exam and 80 Flashcards for quick study

Supplemental Exam Series - Level 5, Level 6, Level 7 & Level 8

♪ 8 Exams to successfully prepare for nationally recognized Theory Exams

UMT Online Courses, Music Theory App & More

♪ UMT Certification Course, Teachers Membership & Elite Educator Program
♪ Ultimate Music Theory App correlates to the Rudiments Workbooks
♪ Free Resources - Teachers Guide, Music Theory Blogs, videos & downloads

Go To: **UltimateMusicTheory.com**

At Ultimate Music Theory we are passionate about helping teachers and students experience the joy of teaching and learning music by creating the most effective music theory materials on the planet!

Introducing the Ultimate Music Theory Family!

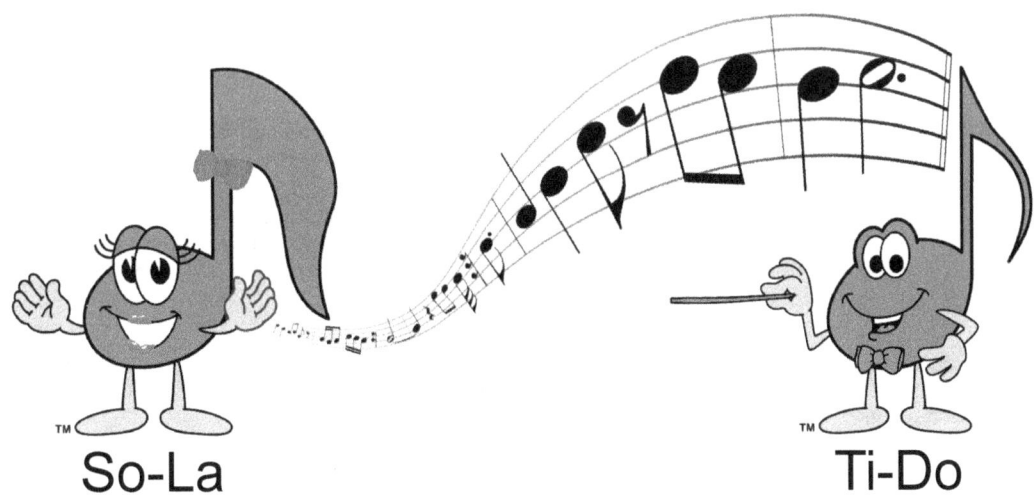

So-La

Meet So-La! So-La loves to sing and dance.

She is expressive, creative and loves to tell stories through music!

So-La feels music in her heart. She loves to teach, compose and perform.

Ti-Do

Meet Ti-Do! Ti-Do loves to count and march.

He is rhythmic, consistent and loves the rules of music theory!

Ti-Do feels music in his hands and feet. He loves to analyze, share tips and conduct.

So-La & Ti-Do will guide you through Mastering Music Theory!

Enriching Lives Through Music Education

The Ultimate Music Theory™ Comparison Chart to the 2016 Royal Conservatory of Music Theory Syllabus.
Level 5

The Ultimate Music Theory™ Rudiments Workbooks, Supplemental Workbooks and Exams prepare students for successful completion of the Royal Conservatory of Music Theory Levels.

UMT Basic Rudiments Workbook plus the LEVEL 4 Supplemental Workbook = RCM Theory Level 4.
♫ Note: Additional completion of the LEVEL 5 Supplemental Workbook = RCM Theory Level 5.

RCM Level 5 Theory Concept	**Ultimate Music Theory Basic Workbook**
Required Keys: - Major and minor keys up to four sharps and flats	**Keys Covered:** - Major and minor keys up to four sharps and flats * Workbook Page - Circle of Fifths Review - Major Key Signatures - Four Sharps and Four Flats * Workbook Page - Circle of Fifths Review - Minor Key Signatures - Four Sharps and Four Flats
Pitch and Notation: - Notes up to and including four ledger lines above and below the Treble Staff and Bass Staff - Enharmonic Equivalents - Transposition of short melodies up or down one octave, including change of clef - Rewriting melodies at the same pitch in the alternate clef (from Treble to Bass or Bass to Treble)	**Pitch and Notation Covered:** - Notes up to and including five ledger lines above and below the Treble Staff and Bass Staff - Same pitch, alternate clef - Enharmonic Equivalents - Transposition of short melodies up or down one octave, including change of clef - Rewriting melodies at the same pitch in the alternate clef (from Treble to Bass or Bass to Treble) * Workbook Pages - Transposition and Rewriting melodies * Workbook Pages - Joining Beams & Stem Direction Review * Workbook Page - Stems and Beams in Two-Part Music * Workbook Page - Rest Placement in Two-Part Music
Rhythm and Meter - Note and Rest Values: breve, whole, half, quarter, eighth, sixteenth notes and rests; dotted whole, dotted half, dotted quarter, dotted eighth notes and rests - Triplets (quarter, eighth, sixteenth notes) - Strong, weak and medium beats - Upbeat (anacrusis) - Time Signatures: 2/4, 3/4, 4/4, 2/8, 3/8, 4/8 - New Time Signatures: 2/2, 3/2, 4/2, 6/8 - Application of Time Signatures, bar lines, notes and rests	**Rhythm and Meter Covered** - Note Values: Breve, Whole, Half, Quarter, Eighth, Sixteenth - Dotted Note Values: Dotted Whole, Dotted Half, Dotted Quarter, Dotted Eighth - Rest Values: Breve, Whole, Half, Quarter, Eighth, Sixteenth * Workbook Page - Note and Rest Value Review * Workbook Pages - The Value of the Dot for Notes and for Rests - Triplets (quarter notes, eighth notes, sixteenth notes) - Pulse: Strong, weak and Medium - Upbeat (anacrusis) - Time Signatures: Simple Time - 2/8, 2/4, 2/2 (Cut Time), 3/8, 3/4, 3/2, 4/8, 4/4 (Common Time), 4/2 * Workbook Pages - Introducing Compound Time and 6/8 Time * Workbook Page - Comparing 3/4 (Simple) and 6/8 (Compound) Time - Application of Time Signatures, bar lines, notes and rests * Workbook Pages - Rhythm and Meter Review - Bar Lines and Rests
Intervals - Chromatic and Diatonic half steps; Whole Steps - Melodic and Harmonic Intervals (Major, minor and Perfect) within an octave, above the Tonic of required Major keys only (using Key Signatures or accidentals)	**Intervals Covered** - Chromatic and Diatonic half steps (semitones); Whole Steps (tones) - Melodic and Harmonic Intervals (Major, minor and Perfect) within an octave, above the Tonic of required Major keys only (using Key Signatures or accidentals) * Workbook Page - Identifying Intervals in Keyboard Style Music * Workbook Page - Identifying Intervals in Two-Part Music * Workbook Page - Parallel Intervals

* Supplemental Workbook Pages - New concepts introduced in the 2016 RCM Theory Syllabus.

RCM Level 5 Theory Concept (Continued)

Scales and Scale Degree Names

- Major and minor scales (natural, harmonic and melodic forms) up to four sharps or flats (using key signatures and/or accidentals)

- Relative Major and minor keys

- Parallel Major and minor keys (up to four sharps or flats)

- Scale Degree Names: Tonic, Subdominant, Dominant, Leading Tone and Subtonic

Chords and Harmony

- Tonic, Subdominant and Dominant Triads of required keys in Root Position and Inversions (solid/blocked or broken form)

- Dominant 7th Chords in Root Position
- Functional Chord Symbols (I, i, IV, iv, V, V^7) in Root Position only
- Root/Quality Chord Symbols (ex. C, Am, G7)

Form and Analysis

- Identification of concepts from this and previous levels within short music examples

- Identification of the key (Major or minor) of a given passage with a Key Signature

- Identification of question-answer phrase pairs (parallel period)

- melodic phrases: same, similar, different (a, a1, b)

Melody and Composition

- Composition of a four-measure answer phrase to a given question phrase in a Major key, creating a parallel period

- Stable and unstable scale degrees

Musical Terms and Signs

- Tempo, Dynamics and Articulation

Music History/Appreciation

Guided Listening: "Hallelujah Chorus" from Messiah by George Frideric Handel. Listening Focus: Oratorio, Chorus (Soprano, Alto, Tenor, Bass)

Guided Listening: "Queen of the Night" ("Der Hölle Rache kocht in meinem Herzen") from The Magic Flute by Wolfgang Amadeus Mozart. Listening Focus: Opera, Aria

Guided Listening: "Over the Rainbow" from The Wizard of Oz by Harold Arlen. Listening Focus: Verse-Chorus structure

Examination
Level 5 Theory Examination

Ultimate Music Theory Basic Workbook (Continued)

Scales and Scale Degree Names Covered

- Major and minor scales (natural, harmonic and melodic forms) up to four sharps or flats (using key signatures and/or accidentals)
* Workbook Page - Scale Review - Key Signatures and Accidentals

- Relative Major and minor keys

* Workbook Pages - Parallel (or "Tonic") Major and minor Keys and Scales

- Scale Degree Names: Tonic, Subdominant, Dominant
* Workbook Pages - Scale Degrees (Tonic, Supertonic, Mediant, Subdominant, Dominant, Submediant, Leading Tone and Subtonic)

Chords and Harmony Covered

- Tonic, Subdominant and Dominant Triads of required keys in Root Position (solid/blocked or broken form)
* Workbook Pages - Identifying Triads in Root Position and Inversions
* Workbook Pages - Writing Triads in Root Position and Inversions
* Workbook Pages - Placement of Accidentals when Writing Triads
* Workbook Page - Triad Review - Root, Quality and Position

* Workbook Pages - Dominant 7th Chords in Root Position
* Workbook Pages - Functional Chord Symbols (I, i, IV, iv, V, V^7) in Root Position only. Bonus Page - Game - Feed the Fish
* Workbook Pages - Root/Quality Chord Symbols (ex. C, Am, G7)

Form and Analysis Covered

- Identification of concepts from this and previous levels within short music examples

- Identification of the key (Major or minor) of a given passage with a Key Signature

* Workbook Pages - Identification of Question & Answer Phrases (Parallel Period)

* Workbook Pages - Identification of Melodic Phrases (a, a1, b)

Melody and Composition Covered

* Workbook Pages - Composition of a four-measure Answer Phrase to a Given Question Phrase to create a Parallel Period (Major key)

* Workbook Pages - Melody writing ending on stable/unstable degrees

Musical Terms and Signs Covered

* Workbook Pages - Musical Terms and Signs
* Workbook Page Bonus - Analysis and Sight Reading

Music History/Appreciation Covered

* Workbook Pages - G. F. Handel & Analysis of Hallelujah Chorus from Messiah Listening Focus: Oratorio - Chorus (SATB)
Free Resources for Listening Activities & Watching Videos

* Workbook Pages - W. A. Mozart & Analysis of Queen of the Night from The Magic Flute Listening Focus: Opera - Aria
Free Resources for Listening Activities & Watching Videos

* Workbook Pages - H. Arlen & Analysis of Over the Rainbow from The Wizard of Oz Listening Focus: Solo Soprano, Verse-Chorus Structure. Free Resources for Listening Activities & Watching Videos

Review Tests & Final Exam

- 12 Accumulative Review Tests (1 with each of the 12 Lessons)
* UMT Level 5 Theory Exam
* UMT Exam Series - Basic Rudiments

Get your **UltimateMusicTheoryApp.com** - Over 7000 Flashcards including audio! Learn Faster with all 6 Subjects: Beginner - Prep, Basic, Intermediate, Advanced, Ear Training & Music Trivia (including History).

NOTE and REST VALUE REVIEW

Each **Note** has a specific time value of sound and can be written at different pitches. Each **Rest** has a specific time value of silence and is always written in the same place on any staff.

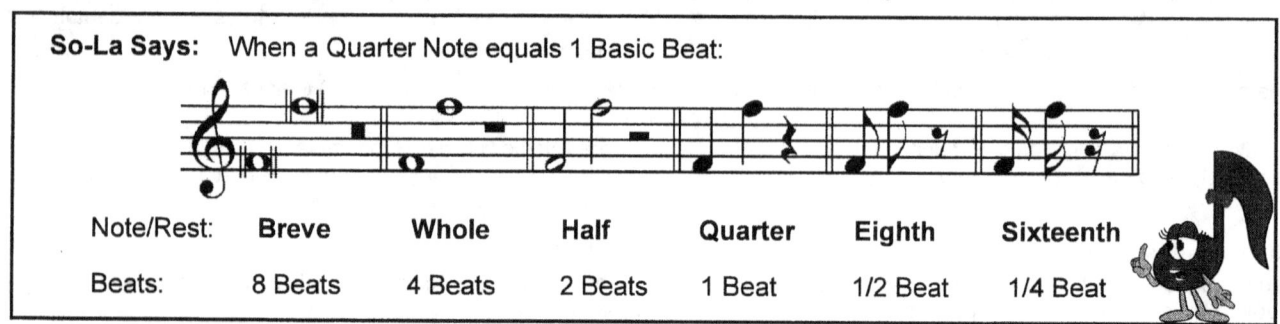

♫ **Ti-Do Tip:** A Breve Note is also called a Double Whole Note. o + o = |o|

A Breve Rest is also called a Double Whole Rest. ▬ + ▬ = ▬▬

1. Write the number of beats for each note.

Beats: __4__ __1__ __¼__ __8__ __½__ __2__ __8__ __¼__

2. Complete the following.

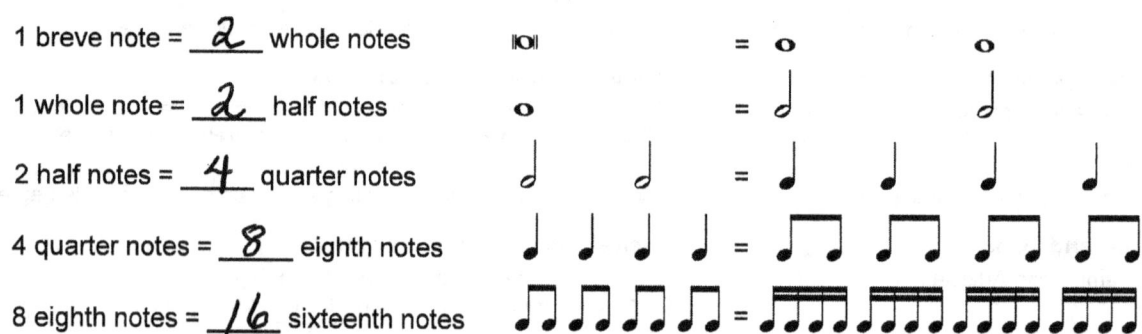

1 breve note = __2__ whole notes

1 whole note = __2__ half notes

2 half notes = __4__ quarter notes

4 quarter notes = __8__ eighth notes

8 eighth notes = __16__ sixteenth notes

RESTS: For all rests, "**Party Space 3**" is the space to be! ▬▬ fits into space 3. ▬ hangs into space 3. ▬ sits up into space 3. 𝄽 top line goes into space 3. 𝄾 and 𝄿 start in space 3.

3. a) Below each bracket, write the rest that has the same time value of silence as the value of the note.
   b) Name each Note/Rest.

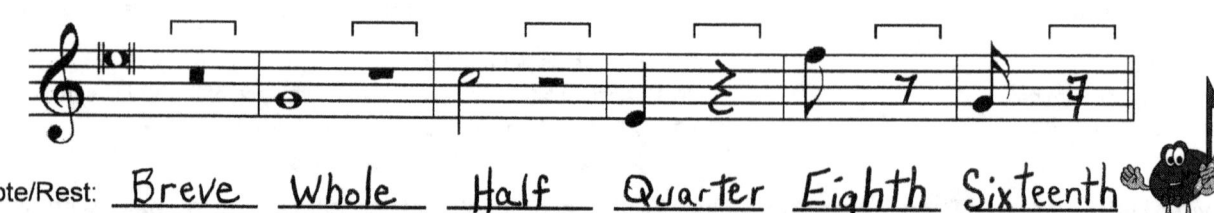

Note/Rest: __Breve__ __Whole__ __Half__ __Quarter__ __Eighth__ __Sixteenth__

THE VALUE OF THE DOT for NOTES and for RESTS

A **Dot** placed after a note adds "**half the value**" of the note. The dot is written behind (after) the note in the same space for a space note, and in the space above for a line note.

So-La Says: When a Quarter Note equals 1 Basic Beat:

Dotted Whole Note	**Dotted Half Note**	**Dotted Quarter Note**	**Dotted Eighth Note**
o· = o + d	d· = d + ♩	♩· = ♩ + ♪	♪· = ♪ + ♬
6 = 4 + 2	3 = 2 + 1	1½ = 1 + ½	¾ = ½ + ¼

♫ **Ti-Do Tip:** When a stem is down, the dot is still written behind (after) the note.

The **dot** is written behind (after) the note in the **same space** for a space note, and in the **space above** for a line note.

1. a) Add a dot to create a dotted note in each measure.
   b) Write the number of beats for each dotted note.

Beats: __6__ __3__ __1½__ __¾__ __6__ __3__ __1½__ __¾__

A **Dot** placed after a rest adds "**half the value**" of the rest.

Dotted Whole Rest	**Dotted Half Rest**	**Dotted Quarter Rest**	**Dotted Eighth Rest**
▬· = ▬ + ▬	▬· = ▬ + 𝄽	𝄽· = 𝄽 + 𝄾	𝄾· = 𝄾 + 𝄿
6 = 4 + 2	3 = 2 + 1	1½ = 1 + ½	¾ = ½ + ¼

The dot is written behind (after) the rest in **space three**. Party Space 3 is the space to be!

There are specific rules regarding the use of Dotted Rests. Dotted Rests should not be used in Simple Time.

2. a) Add a dot in space 3 behind (after) the rest in each measure to create a dotted rest.
   b) Write the number of beats for each dotted rest.

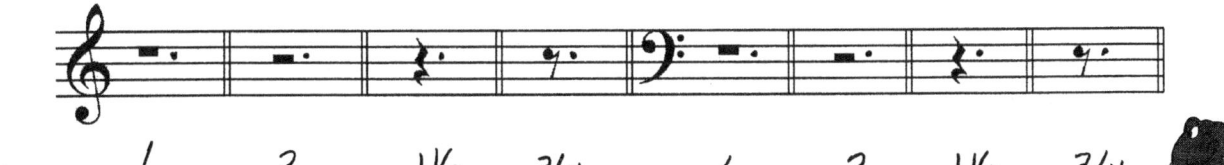

Beats: __6__ __3__ __1½__ __¾__ __6__ __3__ __1½__ __¾__

STEM DIRECTION REVIEW

A **Stem** is approximately **one octave in length**. A stem is written down on the left side of the notehead. A stem is written up on the right side of the notehead.

So-La Says: Follow the Stem Rules! When the notehead is:

ABOVE the middle line, stem DOWN on the left: 'ℙ' like 'p' in → **P**izza
ON the middle line, stem DOWN on the left or UP on the right:
BELOW the middle line, stem UP on the right: 'ⅆ' like 'd' in → **D**onuts

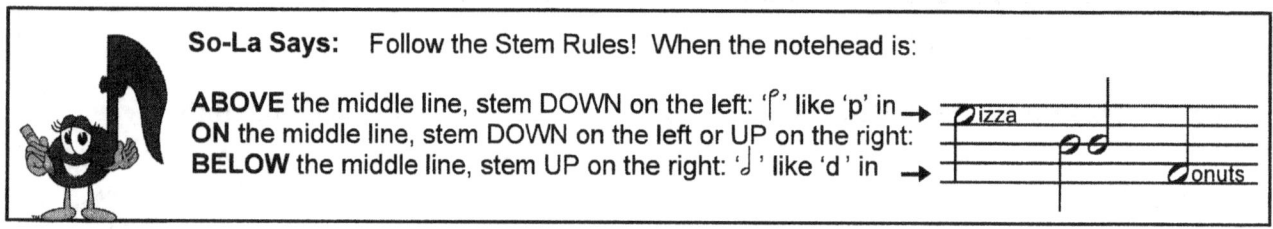

♫ **Ti-Do Tip:** When a note is written on a ledger line, the stem length must be **extended** so that the stem reaches (touches or slightly passes) the **center line** (line 3) of the staff.

1. Add a stem to each notehead to form half notes. Name each note.

C E A F D G B G B F

2. Add a stem to each notehead to form quarter notes. Name each note.

A F G E E G A C D B

FLAGS: For an eighth note or a sixteenth note, the **FLAG** always goes to the **RIGHT**. When writing these, the end of the flag does not touch the notehead.

For notes on **ledger lines**, extend the stem to touch or slightly pass the **center line** (line 3) of the staff.

3. a) In Measure 1, add a stem and a flag to form single eighth notes.
   b) In Measure 2, add a stem and 2 flags to form single sixteenth notes.

JOINING NOTES WITH BEAMS REVIEW

When joining notes with a **Beam** (or Beams), the note furthest away from the third line (the middle line) determines the direction of all the stems.

The **direction of the pitch** between the first note and the last note determines the **beam angle**.

When the first note and the last note are at the same pitch, the beam angle is **Horizontal**. ⟶

When the first note is at a lower pitch then the last note, the beam angle is **Ascending**. ↗

When the first note is at a higher pitch then the last note, the beam angle is **Descending**. ↘

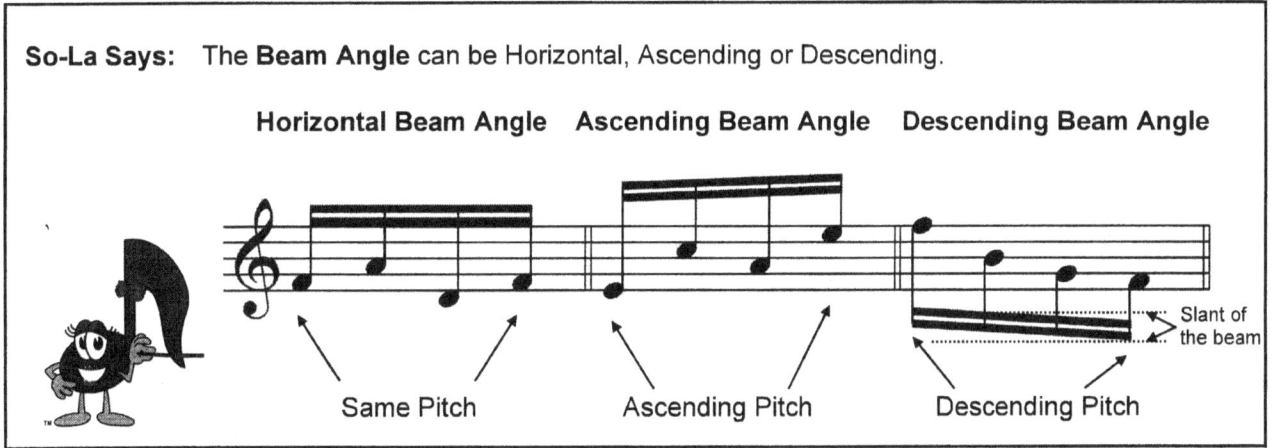

So-La Says: The **Beam Angle** can be Horizontal, Ascending or Descending.

♫ **Ti-Do Tip:** When writing notes with a beam or beams, the shortest stem may end up being less than one octave in length so that the **slant of the beam is approximately one staff space**.

Some stem lengths may need to be longer than one octave to reach and connect to the beam (beams).

When there are 2 or more beams, all stems must extend through all beams to reach the outside beam.

1. a) Observing the pitch between the first note and the last note in each measure (same, ascending or descending), identify the Beam Angle as horizontal, ascending or descending.

   b) Determine the note furthest away from the middle line and add a one-octave long stem to that note. Add a one-octave long stem to all remaining notes in that same direction.

   c) Add beams to create beamed sixteenth notes in each measure. Lengthen any stems as needed to join all 4 sixteenth notes with the correct Beam Angle.

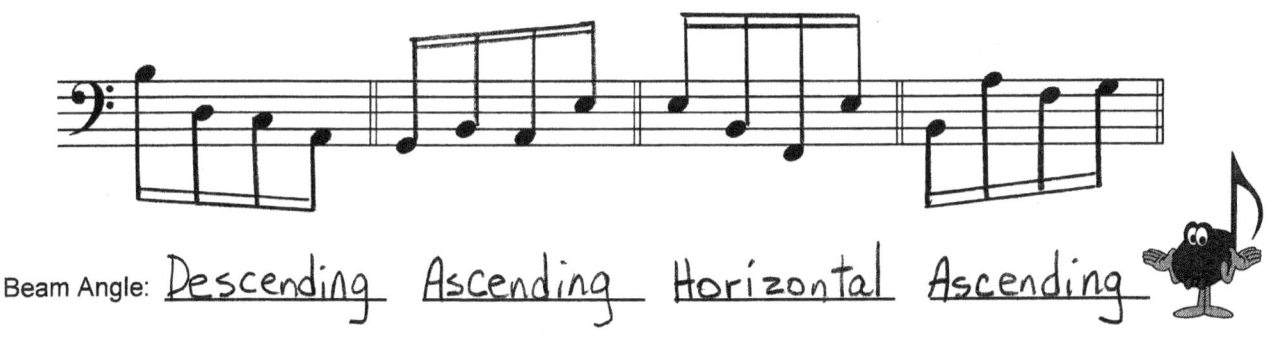

Beam Angle: Descending   Ascending   Horizontal   Ascending

STEMS and BEAMS in TWO-PART MUSIC

In music, **Texture** refers to the type of different musical "voices" in a piece of music. A voice or part usually means a single vocal melody, but it can also mean a single melody on an instrument.

Monophonic Texture - Texture of music with a single "voice" or "part". Also called Monophony.
Polyphonic Texture - Texture of music with two or more independent melodic lines that perform at the same time. Also called Polyphony.

Two-Part Writing or Two-Part Texture is a Polyphonic Texture with 2 different musical voices.
When written on **one staff**: Upper Voice/Part = Stems up; Lower Voice/Part = Stems Down.
When written on **separate staves**: Each Voice/Part follows the Stem Rule.

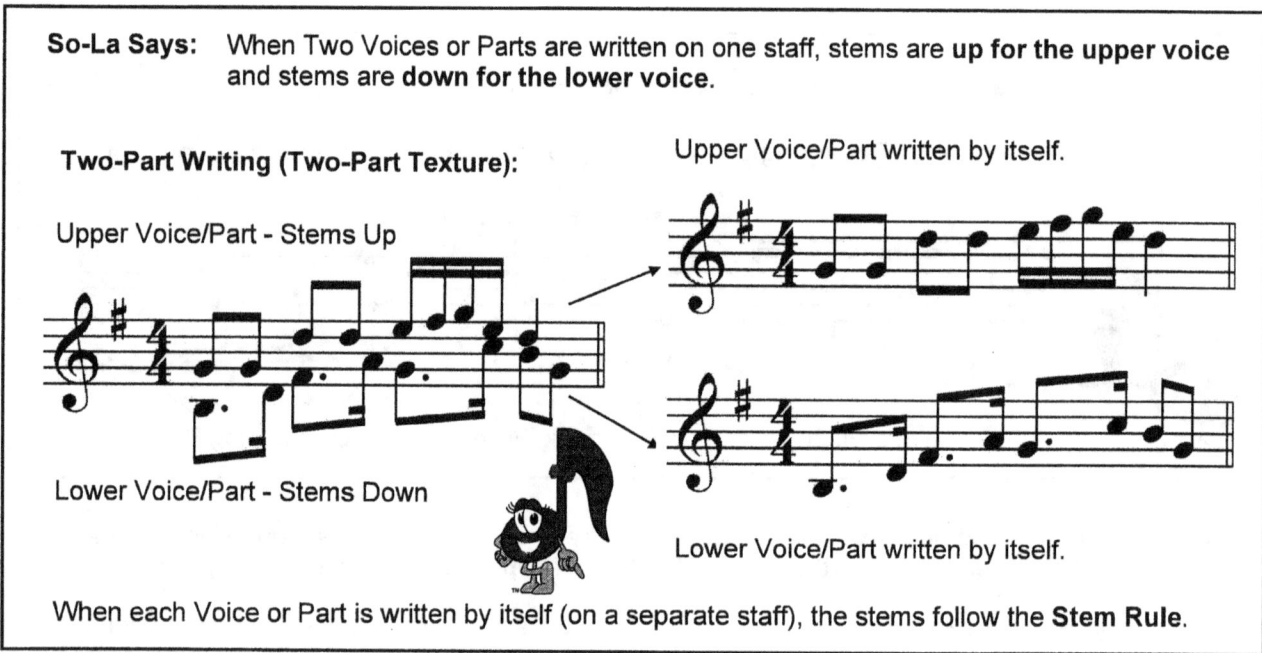

So-La Says: When Two Voices or Parts are written on one staff, stems are **up for the upper voice** and stems are **down for the lower voice**.

When each Voice or Part is written by itself (on a separate staff), the stems follow the **Stem Rule**.

♫ **Ti-Do Tip:** When music is written in Two-Part Texture on one staff, dots for dotted notes are written:
   Upper Voice - in the same space for space notes and in the space above for line notes.
   Lower Voice - in the same space for space notes and in the space below for line notes.

1. The given melody in F Major is written in the Treble Staff in Two-Part Texture (for Two Voices/Parts).
   a) Rewrite the Upper Voice at the same pitch in the upper staff. Follow the Stem Rules.
   b) Rewrite the Lower Voice at the same pitch in the lower staff. Follow the Stem Rules.

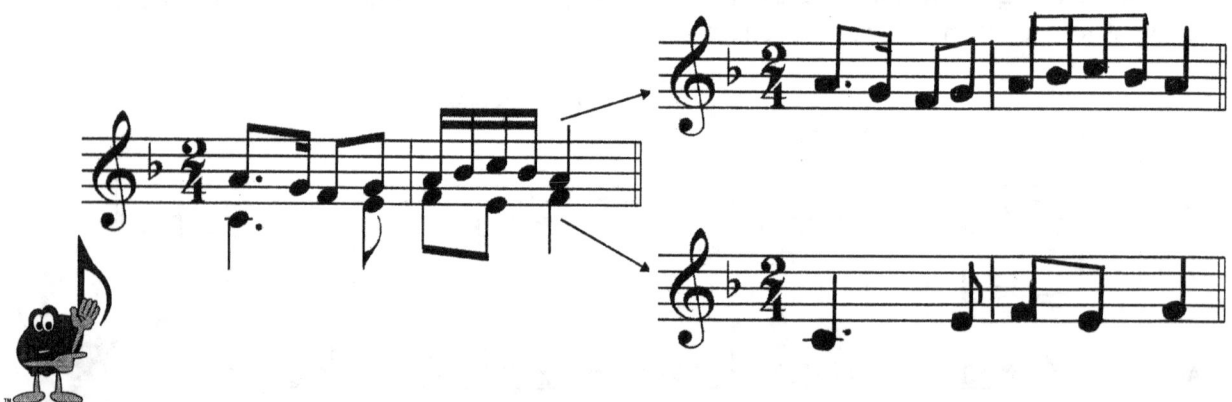

REST PLACEMENT in TWO-PART MUSIC

When writing music in Two-Part Texture on one staff, **rest placement** may be written higher or lower than usual on the staff depending on which voice is having a rest.

When both Voices (Parts) written in the same staff have the same rest, it is preferable to use only one rest (instead of using one rest for each voice).

> **So-La Says:** In Two-Part Writing, rests are written above the staff for the Upper Voice and below the staff for the Lower Voice.
>
> When rewriting each Voice in it's own staff, rests are written in their normal position.

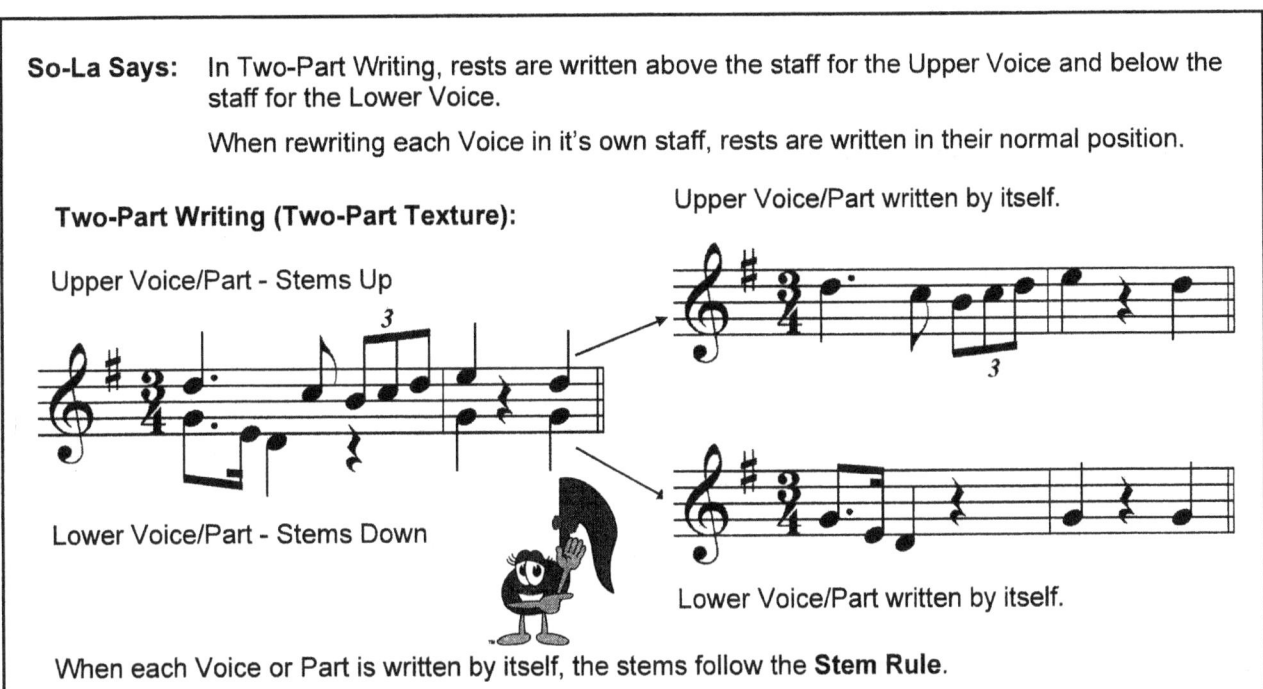

When each Voice or Part is written by itself, the stems follow the **Stem Rule**.

♫ **Ti-Do Tip:** When rewriting Two-Part Music so that each part/voice is written in it's own staff:
   Use the same Clef Sign as the original melody.
   Rewrite the Clef, Key Signature and Time Signature.
   Plan ahead - write in the bar lines before you start rewriting the notes at the same pitch.

1. The given melody in E♭ Major is written in the Treble Staff in Two-Part Texture (for Two Voices/Parts).
   a) Rewrite the Upper Voice at the same pitch in the upper staff. Follow the Stem Rules.
   b) Rewrite the Lower Voice at the same pitch in the lower staff. Follow the Stem Rules.

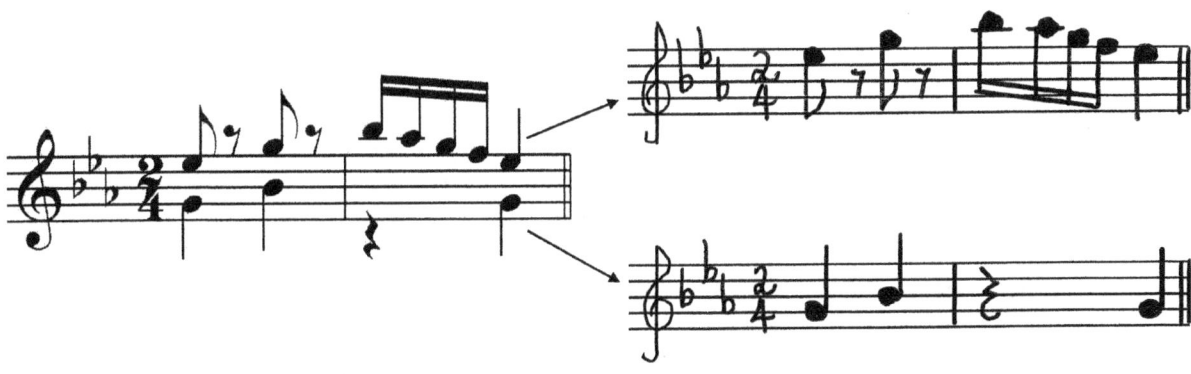

> ♫ **Ti-Do Time:** Play each Two-Part Melody on your Instrument, both parts at the same time. Then play the Upper Voice with your Right Hand and the Lower Voice with your Left Hand. Then play each Single Part Melody, one Voice at a time.

UltimateMusicTheory.com © Copyright 2017 Gloryland Publishing. All Rights Reserved.

INTRODUCTION TO COMPOUND TIME

Time Signatures can be classified as **Simple Time** or **Compound Time**.

So-La Says: Review Simple Time - Duple, Triple and Quadruple in Lesson 8 of the Basic Rudiments Workbook.

The following Chart indicates the Number of beats per measure in Simple and in Compound Time, as well as the value of the Basic Beat.

In **SIMPLE TIME** the top number is **2, 3** or **4**. In **COMPOUND TIME** the top number is **6, 9** or **12**.

SIMPLE TIME	COMPOUND TIME (groups of 3)
Pulse: S = Strong w = weak M = Medium	Compound Dotted Pulse: S• = Sww w• = Mww M• = Mww
Top Number: Number of beats per measure	Top Number: Number of beats per measure
2 S w	6 Sww Mww / S• w•
3 S w w	9 Sww Mww Mww / S• w• w•
4 S w M w	12 Sww Mww Mww Mww / S• w• M• w•
Bottom Number: Basic Beat = 1 count	Bottom Number: Basic Beat = 1 count
Bottom Number / Basic Beat	Bottom Number / Basic Beat / (group of 3) = Compound Basic Beat
2 ♩ (half note)	4 ♩ (♩♩♩) = ♩.
4 ♩	8 ♪ (♪♪♪) = ♩.
8 ♪	16 ♬ (♬♬♬) = ♪.
16 ♬	
Simple Time: Basic Beat = one note (**NO DOT**)	Compound Time: (group of 3) Compound B.B. (Basic Beat) = one **DOTTED** note

1. Identify the Time Signature as Simple (top number is **2, 3** or **4**) or Compound (top number is **6, 9** or **12**).

Simple   Compound   Simple   Compound   Simple   Compound

INTRODUCTION TO 6/8 TIME

In Compound Time: Top Number indicates the number of Basic Beats per measure.
Bottom Number indicates the kind of note that equals one Basic Beat.

In Compound Time, the Basic Beats are in groups of 3. Each group of 3 equals one Compound Basic Beat.

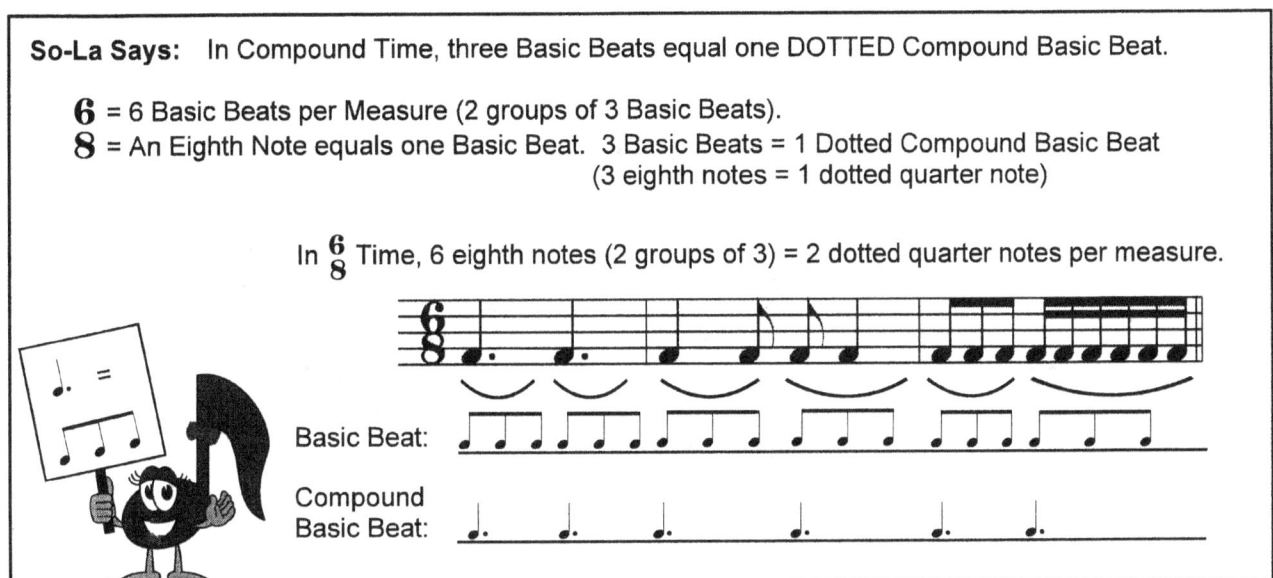

So-La Says: In Compound Time, three Basic Beats equal one DOTTED Compound Basic Beat.

6 = 6 Basic Beats per Measure (2 groups of 3 Basic Beats).
8 = An Eighth Note equals one Basic Beat. 3 Basic Beats = 1 Dotted Compound Basic Beat
(3 eighth notes = 1 dotted quarter note)

In 6/8 Time, 6 eighth notes (2 groups of 3) = 2 dotted quarter notes per measure.

♪ **Ti-Do Tip:** In Compound Time, the Bottom Number 8 = Basic Beat is an Eighth Note.
Three Eighth Notes = One Compound Basic Basic (Dotted Quarter Note).

1. The following rhythms are in Compound Time.
    a) Write the Basic Beat (three eighth notes beamed together) below each Scoop.
    b) Write the Compound Basic Beat (one dotted quarter note) below the Basic Beats.

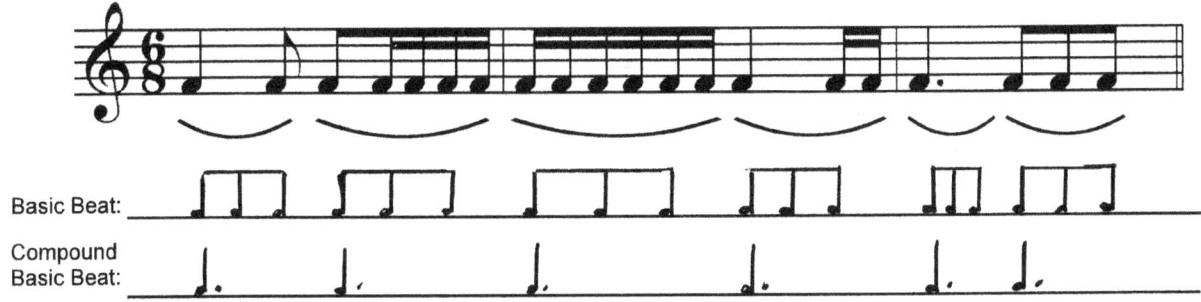

RESTS in 6/8 TIME

In Compound time, a **Dotted Rest** is used to combine all three pulses of the Compound Basic Beat into one rest. Remember that the dot for a dotted rest is always written in **space number 3**.

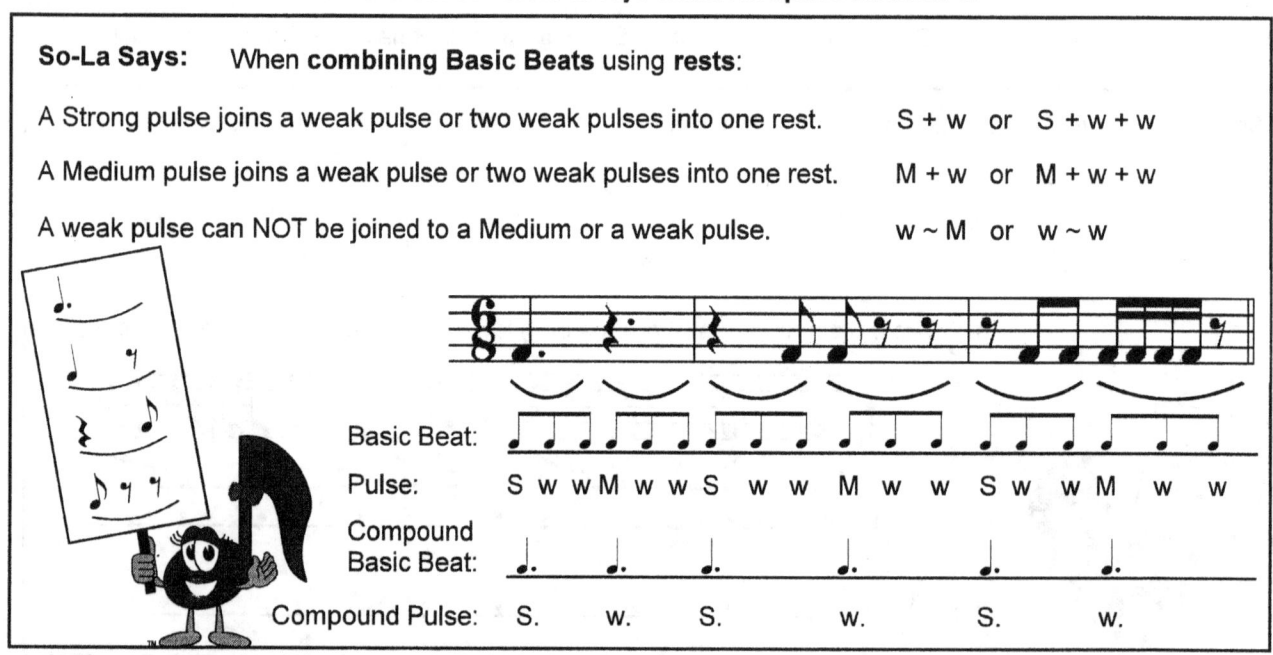

So-La Says: When **combining Basic Beats** using **rests**:

A Strong pulse joins a weak pulse or two weak pulses into one rest.   S + w or S + w + w

A Medium pulse joins a weak pulse or two weak pulses into one rest.   M + w or M + w + w

A weak pulse can NOT be joined to a Medium or a weak pulse.   w ~ M or w ~ w

♪ **Ti-Do Tip:** **Plus (+) sign:** **join** the S + w (+ w) and M + w (+ w)
Tilde (~) sign: do **NOT** join the w ~ M or w ~ w

1. a) Write the Basic Beat and pulse AND the Compound Basic Beat and pulse below each measure.
   b) Add rests below each bracket to complete the measure.
   c) Cross off the Basic Beat and the Compound B.B. (Basic Beat) as each beat is completed.

COMPARING 3/4 (SIMPLE) TIME and 6/8 (COMPOUND) TIME

In **Simple Time**, the **Basic Beat** can be subdivided into two pulses: ♩ = ♩ ♩; ♩ = ♪ ♪; and ♪ = ♬

In **Compound Time**, the **Compound Basic Beat** can be subdivided into three pulses: ♩. = ♪ ♪ ♪

Always line up each Basic Beat directly below the corresponding note or rest on the staff.

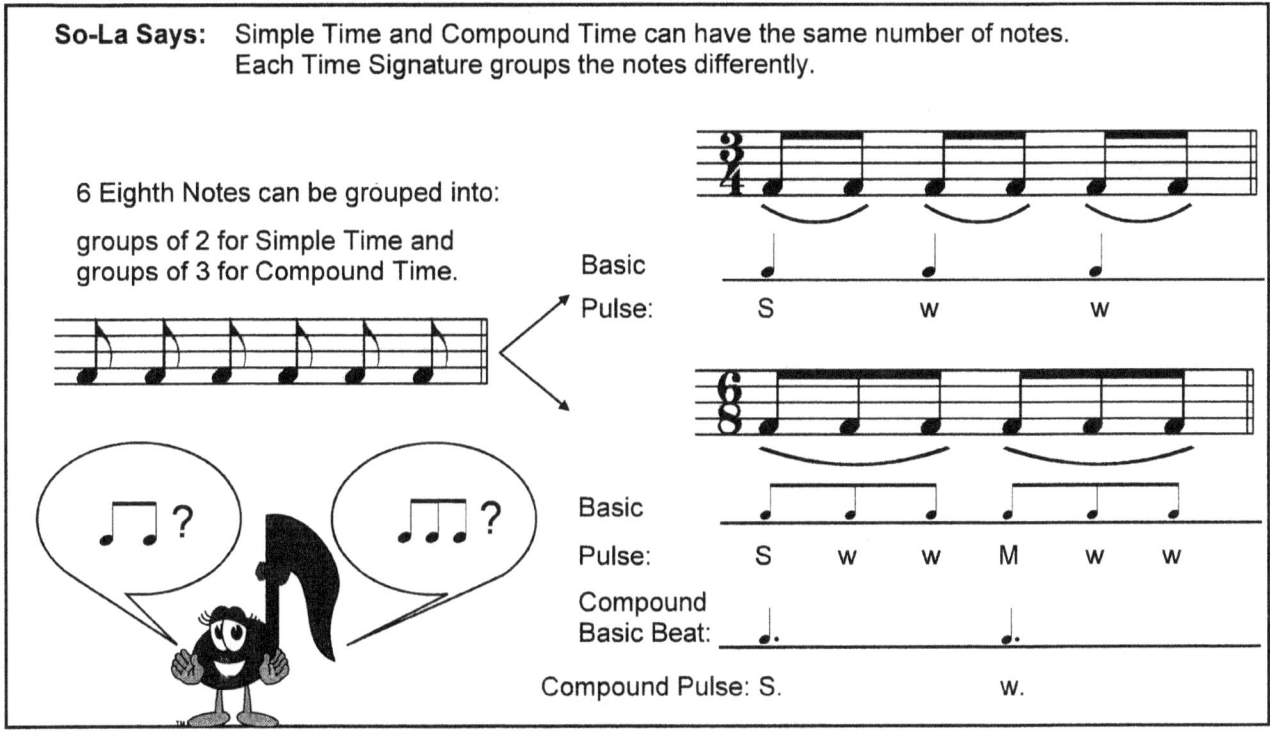

♫ **Ti-Do Tip:** 3 Steps to identify the correct Time Signature:

Step #1: Look for the patterns of notes beamed in groups of 2 or 3.
Step #2: Listen as you count aloud and clap the rhythm. Hear the counts to match the group.
Step #3: Count aloud and play or tap the rhythm. Feel the rhythmic pulse.

1. Add the correct Time Signature below the bracket for each of the following rhythms.

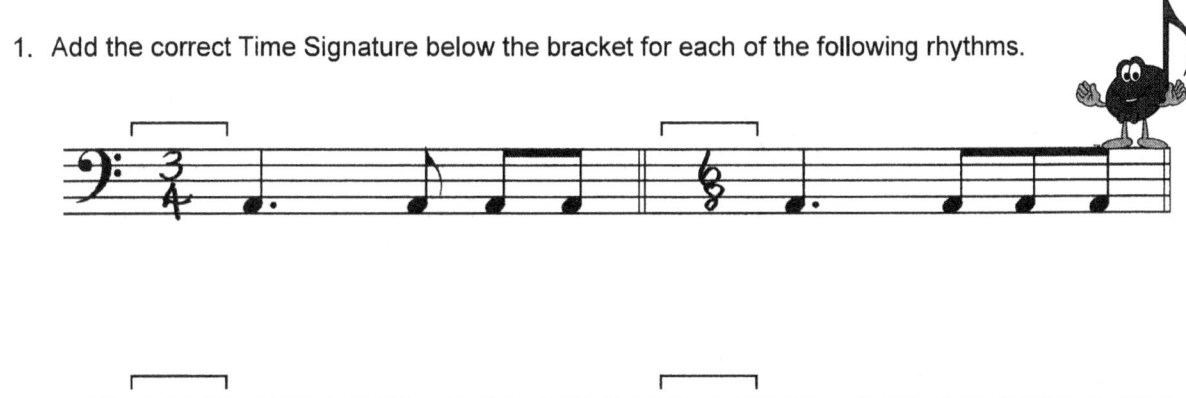

RHYTHM and METER REVIEW - BAR LINES

When adding **Bar Lines**, look for equal groups of the Basic Beat. Determine how many Basic Beats are in a measure. The first measure may be an anacrusis (incomplete measure).

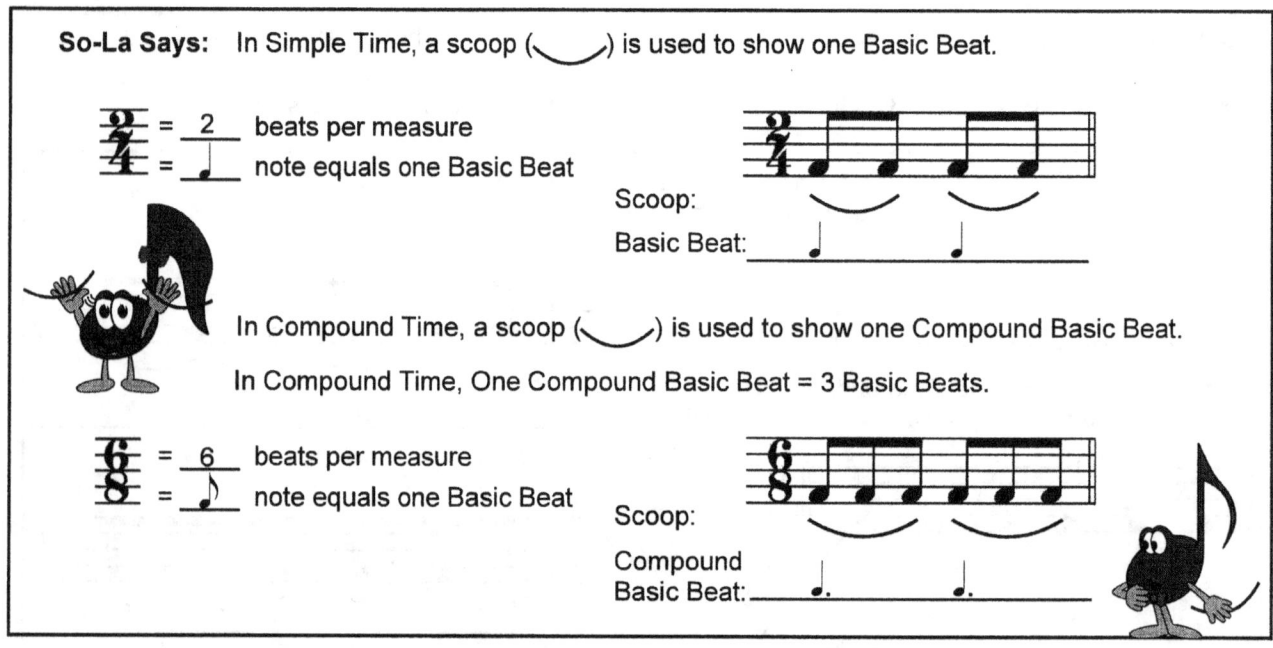

♫ **Ti-Do Tip:** A **Whole Rest** is used for a whole measure of silence in every Time Signature except for $\frac{4}{2}$, where a **Breve Rest** is used for a whole measure of silence.

1. a) Observing the Time Signature, scoop each Basic Beat (or Compound Basic Beat). Write the Basic Beat (or Compound Basic Beat) below each scoop.
   b) Add bar lines.

RHYTHM and METER REVIEW - RESTS

When adding **Rests**, determine if the Time Signature is Simple Time or Compound Time. Then determine if the Basic Beat is an eighth note, quarter note or half note.

So-La Says: When adding rests to a measure, each Basic Beat must be completed before adding rests to fill in any additional Basic Beats with silence.

Simple Time

When adding rests after a given note, add forward:

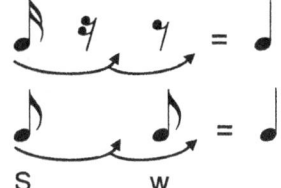

When adding rests before a given note, add backward:

Compound Time

When adding rests after a given note, add forward:

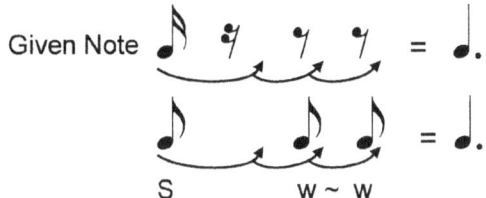

When adding rests before a given note, add backward:

♫ **Ti-Do Tip:** A Dotted Quarter Rest is used only for a complete Compound Basic Beat of silence in $\frac{6}{8}$.

1. a) Write the Basic Beat and pulse (and the Compound Basic Beat and pulse) below each measure.
   b) Add rests below each bracket to complete the measure.
   c) Cross off the Basic Beat (and the Compound B.B.) as each beat is completed.

CIRCLE OF FIFTHS REVIEW - MAJOR KEY SIGNATURES - FOUR SHARPS and FOUR FLATS

The **Circle of Fifths** is a map of the Major and minor Key Signatures. It identifies the number of flats and sharps found in each key. The distance from one key to the next key around the Circle of Fifths is a fifth. Each fifth is 5 letter names and 7 half steps (semitones).

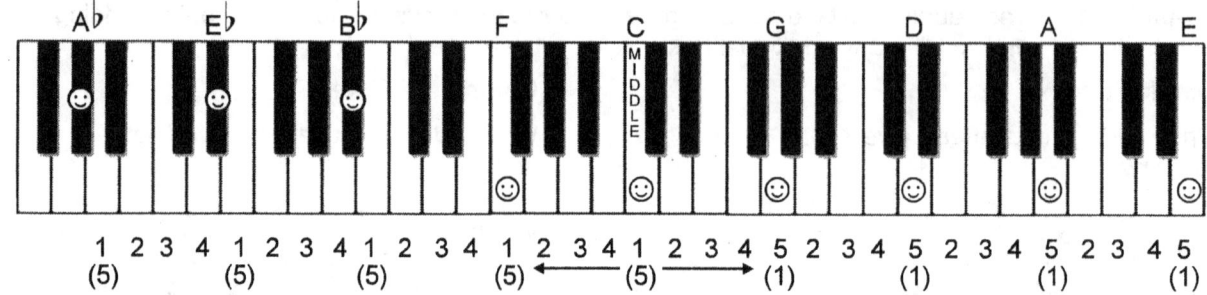

When moving UP from C the fifth note is counted again as (1).   1 ⟶ 5 (1)
When moving DOWN from C the first note is counted again as (5).   1 ⟵ 1 (5)

So-La Says: The Circle of Fifths maps out the Major keys up to and including 4 sharps and 4 flats.

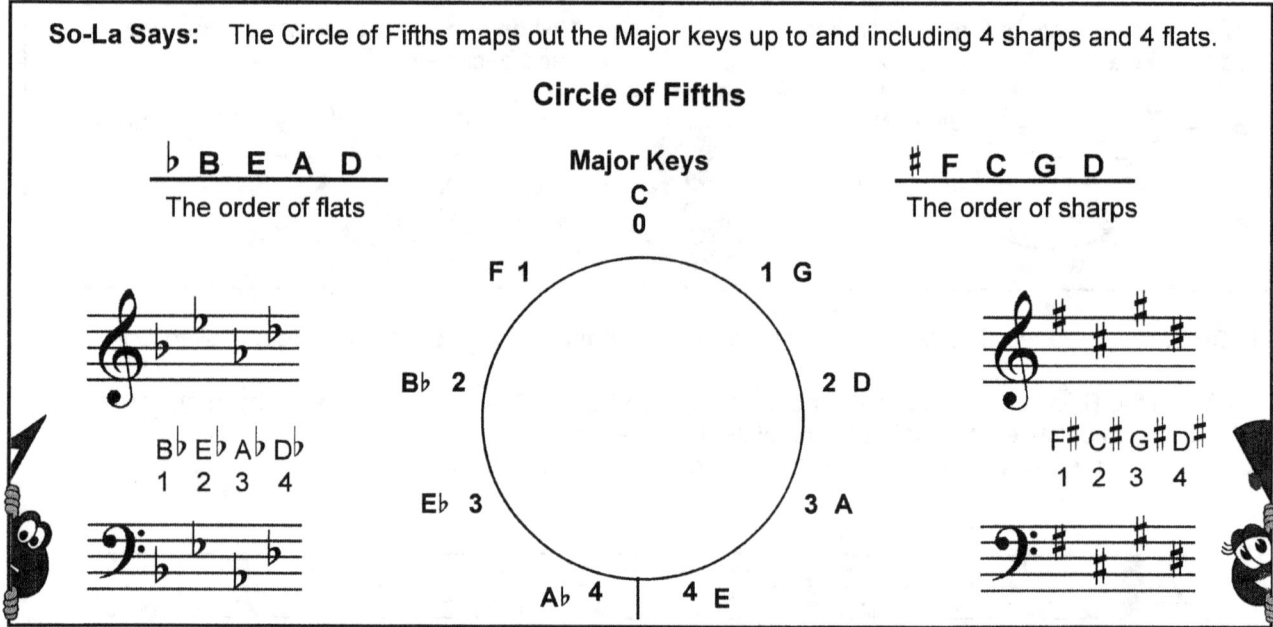

♪ **Ti-Do Tip:** A sharp or flat in a Key Signature applies to all notes, on the staff or using ledger lines, with that letter name.

1. a) Name the notes.
   b) Name the Major key for the following Key Signatures.

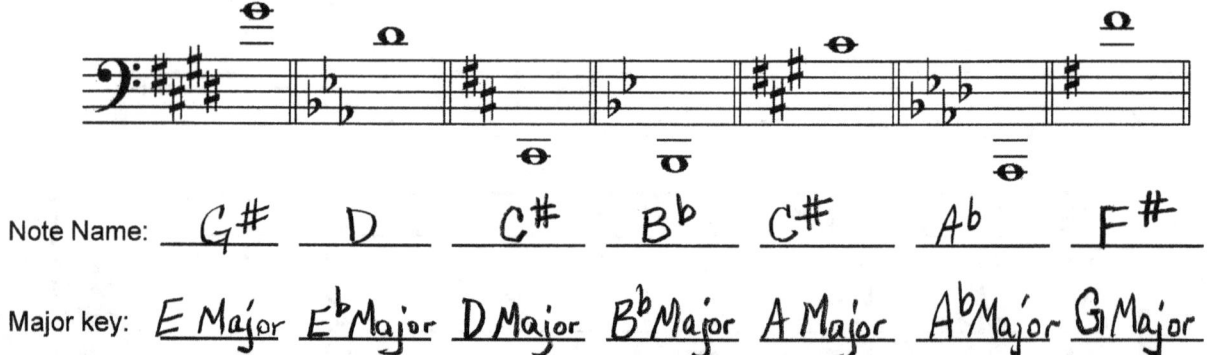

Note Name: G#, D, C#, B♭, C#, A♭, F#

Major key: E Major, E♭ Major, D Major, B♭ Major, A Major, A♭ Major, G Major

CIRCLE OF FIFTHS REVIEW - MINOR KEY SIGNATURES - FOUR SHARPS and FOUR FLATS

Major keys and their relative minor keys share the same **Key Signature**. The minor key is three half steps (semitones) and three letter names (a minor third) below its relative Major.

♫ **Ti-Do Tip:** From the Major key to its relative minor, go **DOWN** 3 half steps (a minor third).
From the minor key to its relative Major, go **UP** 3 half steps (a minor third).

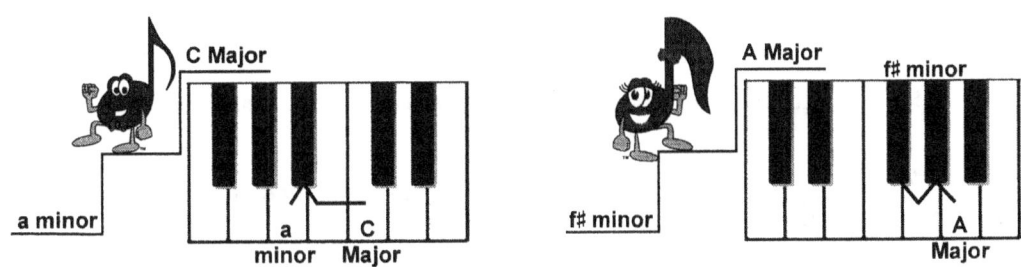

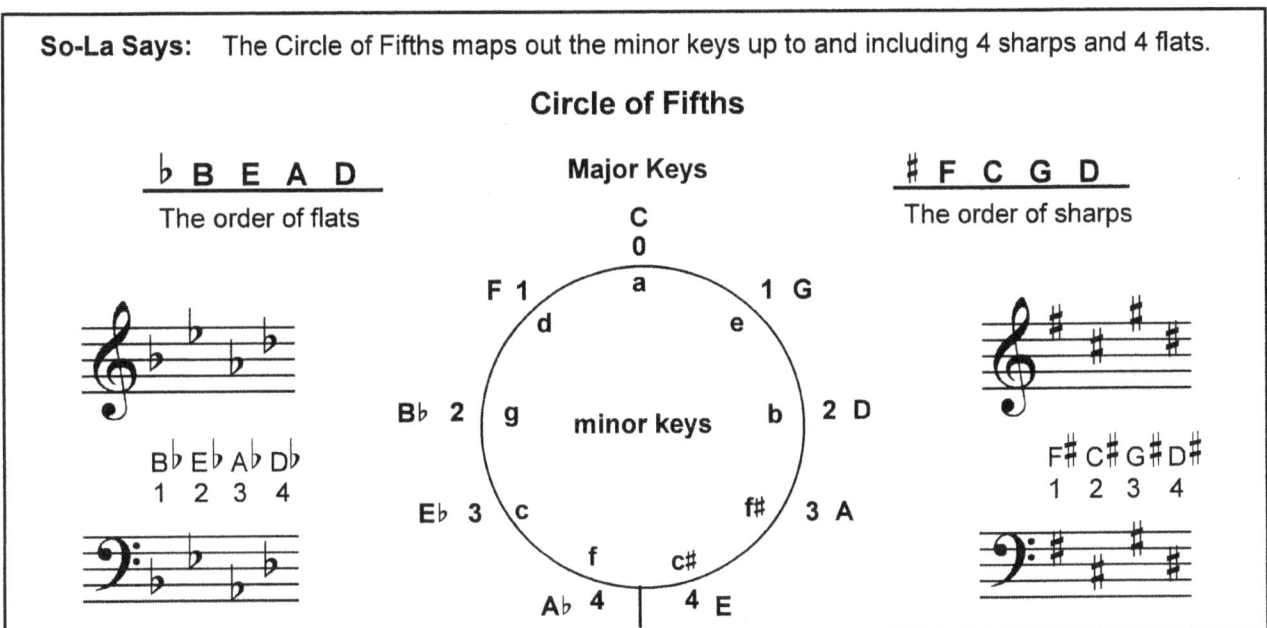

An upper case letter is used when identifying the Major key. The abbreviation for Major is Maj. (C Maj.)
A lower case letter is used when identifying the minor key. The abbreviation for minor is min. (c min.)

1. Name the Major key and its relative minor key for each of the following Key Signatures.

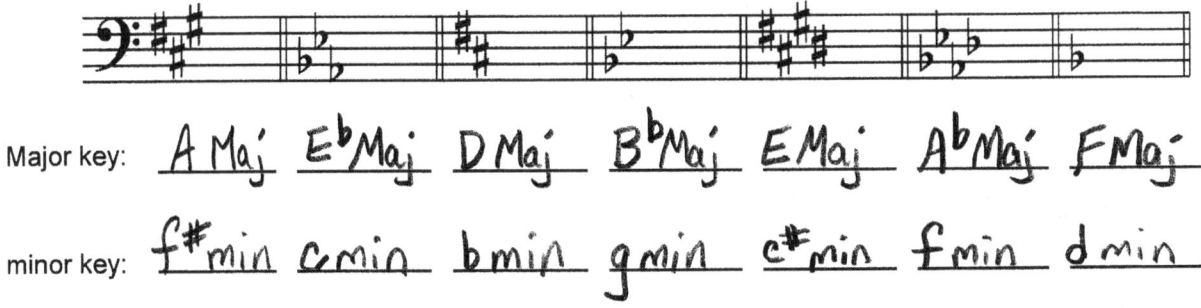

Major key: A Maj, E♭ Maj, D Maj, B♭ Maj, E Maj, A♭ Maj, F Maj

minor key: f# min, c min, b min, g min, c# min, f min, d min

SCALE REVIEW - WRITING SCALES USING a KEY SIGNATURE

A **Scale** is a series of 8 notes in a specific pattern. A scale can be written using a **Key Signature** - the sharps or flats from the Scale Patterns are placed in a specific order at the beginning of the staff.

> **So-La Says:** Major Keys and their relative minor keys share the same Key Signature. The Key Signature is written directly after the Clef Sign.
>
> The minor scale starts on the sixth scale degree of its relative Major Scale.
>
>
>
> **N**   **Natural** minor scale - Nothing added. No extra accidentals.
>
> **H**   **Harmonic** minor scale - Raise the 7th note ascending and descending. (Find the 7 in the H)
>
> **M**   **Melodic** minor scale - Raise the 6th and 7th notes ascending and lower the 6th and 7th notes descending. (Find the 6 and 7 in the M)

♪ **Ti-Do Tip:** When writing scales using a Key Signature, accidentals are found only in the Harmonic minor scale and in the Melodic minor scale.

1. Write the following scales, ascending and descending. Use the correct Key Signature and any necessary accidentals. Use whole notes. Observe the Clef Sign.

   a) E Major scale

   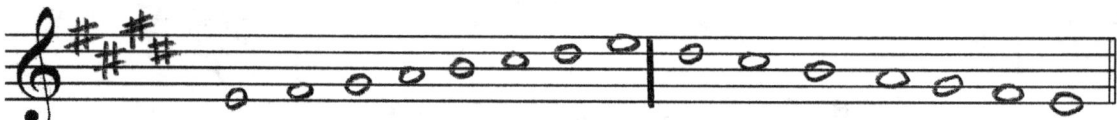

   b) c# minor natural scale

   c) c# minor harmonic scale

   d) c# minor melodic scale

SCALE REVIEW - WRITING SCALES USING ACCIDENTALS

A **Scale** is a series of 8 notes in a specific pattern. A scale can be written using **Accidentals** - the sharps or flats from the Scale Patterns are written on the staff in front of the appropriate notes.

> **So-La Says:** Natural signs are used only to cancel an actual accidental that appears in the scale.
>
> The key of c minor has 3 flats. When writing the c minor melodic scale using accidentals, natural signs are not required to raise the 6th and 7th notes in the ascending melodic minor scale.
>
> Review how to write and use Accidentals in Lesson 2 in the **Basic Rudiments Workbook**.

♪ **Ti-Do Tip:** Scales can be written with or without a center bar line. Always write scales in the same way, either with or without a center bar line.

1. Write the following scales, ascending and descending. Use accidentals. Use whole notes. Observe the Clef Sign.

   a) E♭ Major scale

   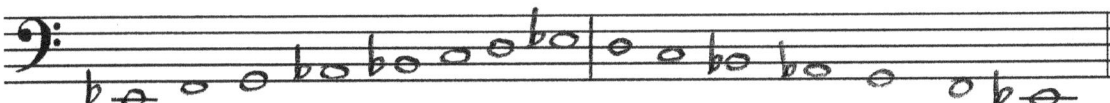

   b) c minor natural scale

   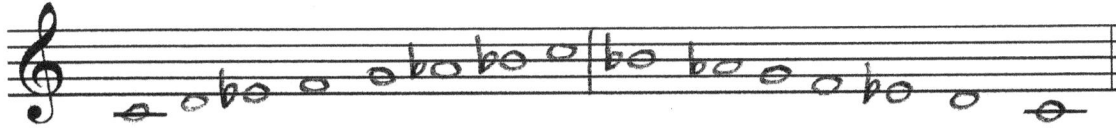

   c) c minor harmonic scale

   d) c minor melodic scale

   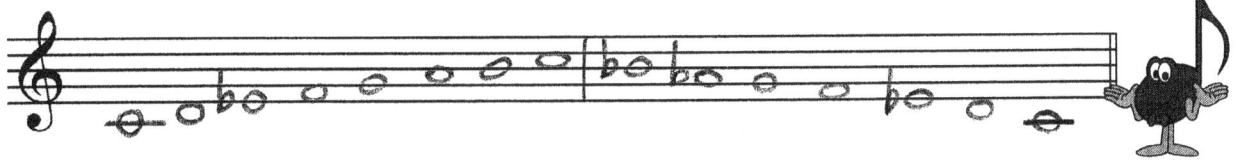

SCALE DEGREES and TECHNICAL DEGREE NAMES

Scale Degree Numbers are numbers with a circumflex, caret sign or hat (ˆ) written above the number.

Technical Degree Names are names used to identify the degrees of a scale.

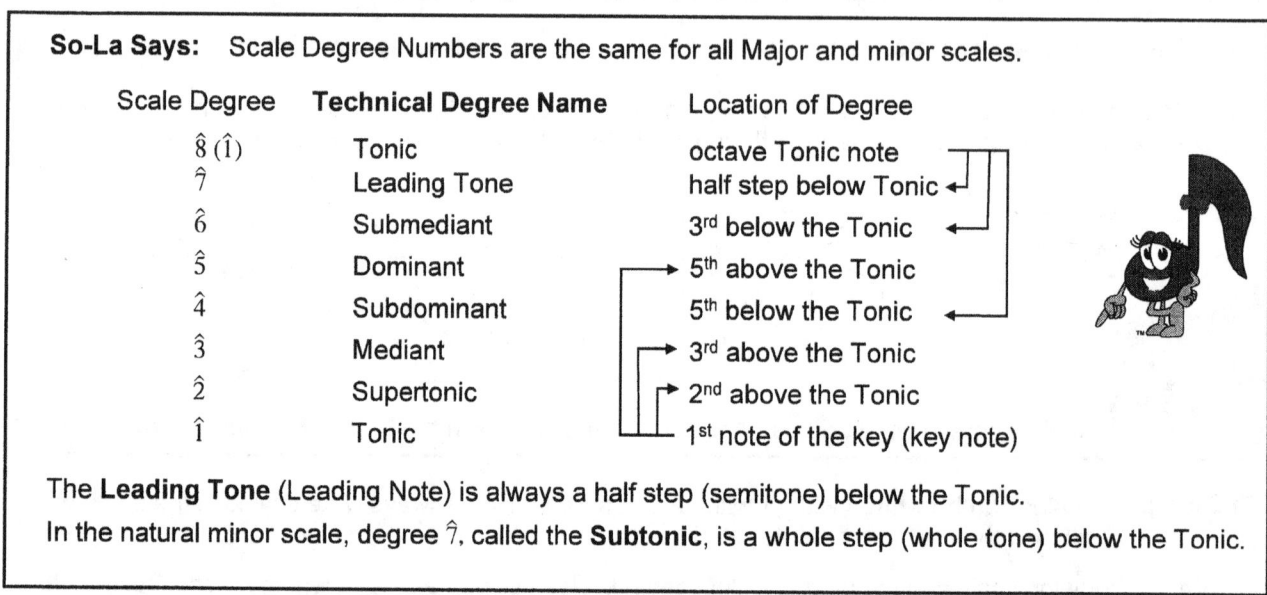

So-La Says: Scale Degree Numbers are the same for all Major and minor scales.

Scale Degree	Technical Degree Name	Location of Degree
$\hat{8}$ ($\hat{1}$)	Tonic	octave Tonic note
$\hat{7}$	Leading Tone	half step below Tonic
$\hat{6}$	Submediant	3rd below the Tonic
$\hat{5}$	Dominant	5th above the Tonic
$\hat{4}$	Subdominant	5th below the Tonic
$\hat{3}$	Mediant	3rd above the Tonic
$\hat{2}$	Supertonic	2nd above the Tonic
$\hat{1}$	Tonic	1st note of the key (key note)

The **Leading Tone** (Leading Note) is always a half step (semitone) below the Tonic.

In the natural minor scale, degree $\hat{7}$, called the **Subtonic**, is a whole step (whole tone) below the Tonic.

♪ **Ti-Do Tip:** Scale Degree $\hat{7}$ in the descending Melodic minor scale is also called the Subtonic as it is a whole step (whole tone) below the Tonic.

1. a) Name the minor key.
   b) Name the Technical Degree Name as the Leading Tone or as the Subtonic.

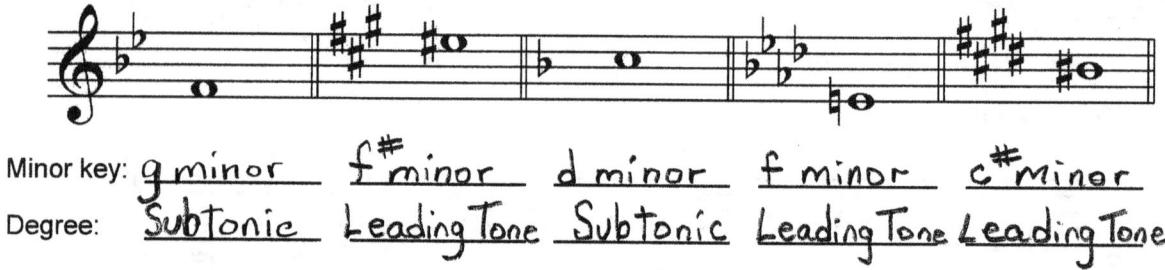

Minor key: g minor, f# minor, d minor, f minor, c# minor
Degree: Subtonic, Leading Tone, Subtonic, Leading Tone, Leading Tone

2. a) Write the Key Signature for the minor key in each measure.
   b) Write the note for the Technical Degree Name in the Bass Staff. Use a whole note.
   c) Write the Scale Degree Number for each note.

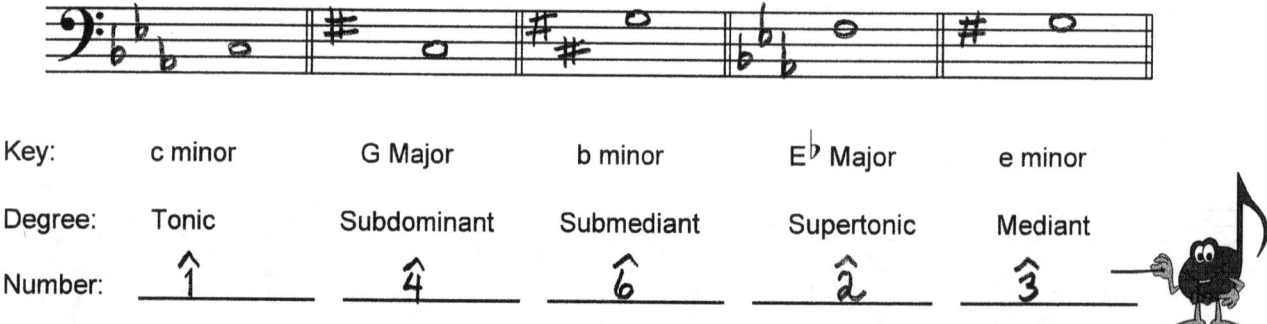

Key: c minor, G Major, b minor, E♭ Major, e minor
Degree: Tonic, Subdominant, Submediant, Supertonic, Mediant
Number: $\hat{1}$, $\hat{4}$, $\hat{6}$, $\hat{2}$, $\hat{3}$

PARALLEL KEYS and RELATIVE KEYS

Parallel Keys share the same Tonic note. D Major and d minor are Parallel Keys. They share the same Tonic note, "D". They do not share the same Key Signature.

Relative Keys share the same Key Signature. D Major and b minor are Relatives. They share the same Key Signature, 2 sharps. They do not share the same Tonic notes.

♪ **Ti-Do Tip:** Parallel Keys are also called "**Tonic Major**" and "**Tonic minor**" keys.
The Tonic Major key of d minor is D Major. The Tonic minor key of D Major is d minor.

1. Fill in the blanks.

   a) The Parallel Major key (Tonic Major key) of c minor is __C__ Major.

   b) The Relative Major key of c minor is __Eb__ Major.

   c) The Parallel minor key (Tonic minor key) of A Major is __a__ minor.

   d) The Relative minor key of A Major is __f#__ minor.

2. Write the following scales, ascending and descending. Use a Key Signature and any necessary accidentals. Use whole notes.

   a) The Relative Major scale of d minor in the Bass Clef. (F Major)

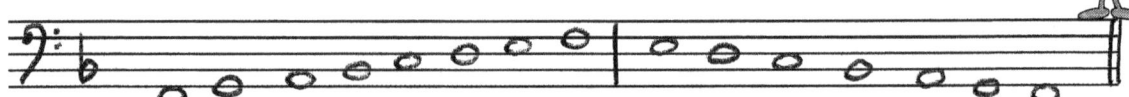

   b) The Parallel minor scale (Tonic minor) harmonic form of F Major in the Treble Clef. (f min harm)

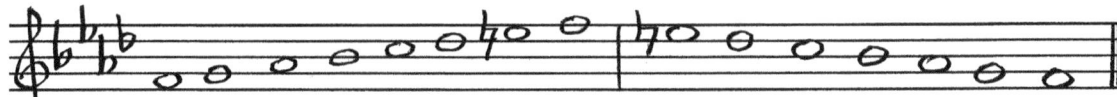

   c) The Parallel minor scale (Tonic minor) melodic form of D Major in the Treble Clef. (d min mel)

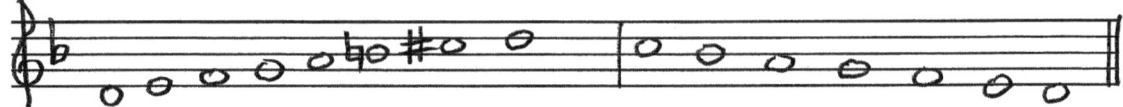

IDENTIFYING INTERVALS using ACCIDENTALS

An Interval is the distance in pitch between two notes. An interval is defined by a **Number** and a **Quality**.

Size or Number: Number of note names counting from the bottom (lower) note to the higher (upper) note.
Quality or Type: Whether the sound created is Major, minor or Perfect.

Interval Quality (Type) is determined by using the Major scale (Major key) of the lower note of the interval. An Interval can be written as a Melodic Interval (separate) or as a Harmonic Interval (together).

Accidentals are taught in Lesson 2 and **Intervals** are taught in Lesson 5 of the **Basic Workbook**. It is important to complete your Basic Workbook and your **UMT Level 4 Supplemental Workbook** before completing your **Level 5 Supplemental Workbook**.

So-La Says: An Accidental placed in front of a note applies to any note that is written on that line or in that space until it is canceled by either another accidental or by a bar line.

The Interval at **A**:

Lower Note: D   Upper Note: F♯

Major Key (of Lower Note): D Major

Key Signature (of Lower Note): F♯ C♯

Interval Name: Major 3

The Interval at **B**:

Lower Note: D   Upper Note: F

Major Key (of Lower Note): D Major

Key Signature (of Lower Note): F♯ C♯

Interval Name: minor 3

An accidental applies only to the notes on the line or in the space where it is written. It does not apply to notes that have the same letter name but appear at a higher or lower position (pitch) on the staff.

♫ **Ti-Do Tip:** A minor interval is one chromatic half step (semitone) smaller than a Major interval.

1. Following the example, name the intervals by completing the following:

Interval note names: (lower note first)	E♭ G	E♭ G♭	E G♯	E G	A♭ C	A♮ C♯
Major key of the lower note:	E♭ Maj	E♭ Maj	E Maj	E Maj	A♭ Maj	A Maj
Key Signature: (of lower note)	B♭ E♭ A♭	B♭ E♭ A♭	F♯ C♯ G♯ D♯	F♯ C♯ G♯ D♯	B♭ E♭ A♭ D♭	F♯ C♯ G♯
Interval name:	Maj 3	min 3	Maj 3	min 3	Maj 3	Maj 3

IDENTIFYING INTERVALS using KEY SIGNATURES

An Interval can be written using accidentals or using a Key Signature.

When naming intervals with a Key Signature, count the number of lines and spaces from one note to the other note (the distance) to determine the interval number (1, 2, 3, etc.). When naming the notes of the interval, observe the Key Signature and any accidentals in the measure that may affect the given notes.

The **Key Signature** of the melody will affect **all the notes** on the staff and on ledger lines.

So-La Says: A **change of key** (changing from one Key Signature to another) is indicated by a thin double bar line (2 thin bar lines) followed by the new Key Signature.

In the **traditional** (old-fashioned) method, each accidental from the original Key Signature was canceled by a natural sign before the new Key Signature was written.

The new **preferred** method is to simply write the new Key Signature after the bar lines.

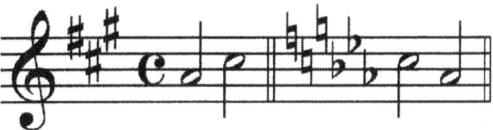

When the new key is **C Major** or **a minor**, it is necessary to cancel the old Key Signature by using natural signs for each sharp or flat indicated in the old Key Signature.

♪ **Ti-Do Tip:** The function of the Naturals used to cancel a Key Signature is to simply cancel the previous Key Signature. These Naturals **do not** have to be written beside the letter names.

1. Following the example, name the intervals by completing the following:

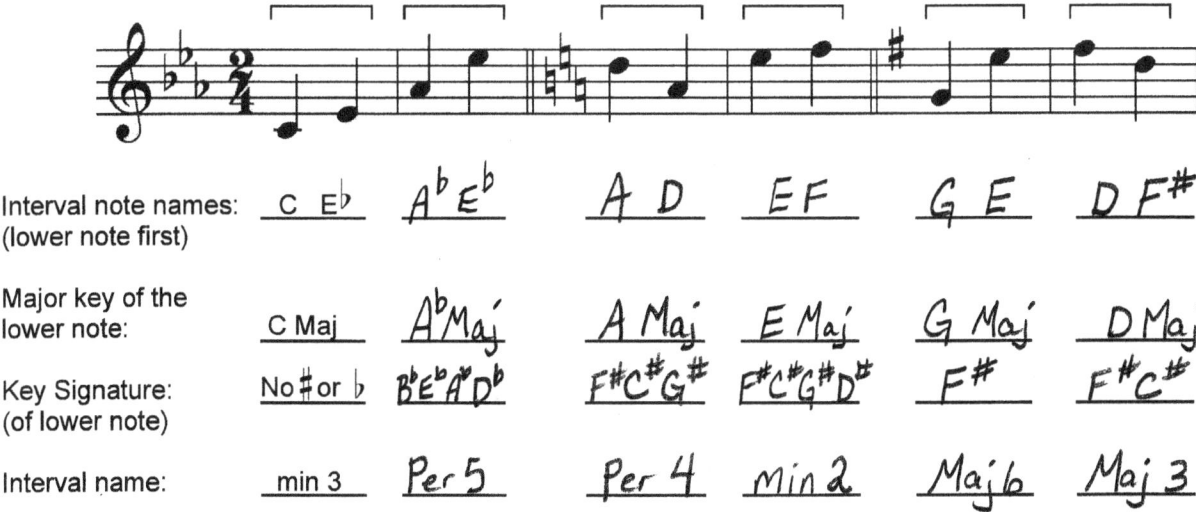

♪ **Ti-Do Time:** LISTEN as your Teacher plays the intervals on Pages 26 and 27.

Identify if the interval has been played as ascending or descending. Name the interval.

IDENTIFYING INTERVALS in MONOPHONIC and in HOMOPHONIC TEXTURE

Monophonic Texture: One melodic line (melody), no accompaniment. A single-voice texture, one part or voice, that is written on one staff. Stems for all notes follow the Stem Rule. Intervals are written as Melodic.

Homophonic Texture: One melodic line (melody), with harmonic blocks (harmony). A single-voice texture with one or more parts/voices written below the melody, using the same rhythm to create Harmonic Intervals. Stems follow the stem rule (one stem per note/harmonic interval). This is called **Single Stemming**.

On the Grand Staff, **Homophonic Texture** is a single line of melody supported by harmonic accompaniment (a single melody in one staff with chords, or "chordal" accompaniment, in the other). Stems for all notes follow the Stem Rule. Intervals are written as both Melodic and Harmonic.

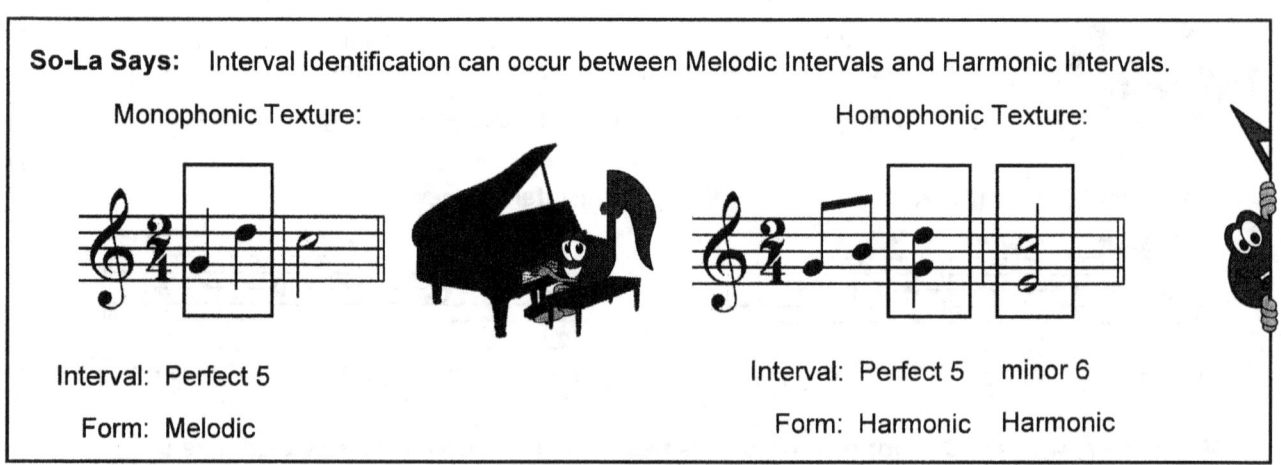

So-La Says: Interval Identification can occur between Melodic Intervals and Harmonic Intervals.

Monophonic Texture:
Interval: Perfect 5
Form: Melodic

Homophonic Texture:
Interval: Perfect 5   minor 6
Form: Harmonic   Harmonic

♪ **Ti-Do Tip:** An Interval is always based on the notes of the Major scale of the lower note.

1. The following is the opening theme from G.P. Telemann's Fantasia in C Major.

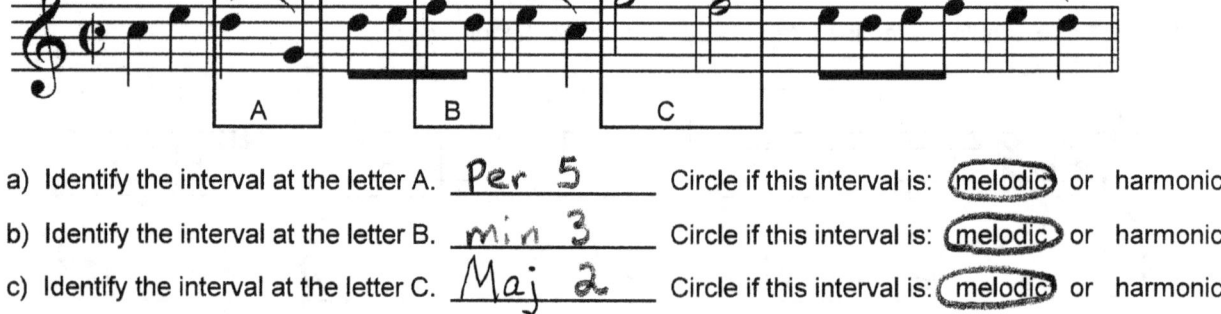

   a) Identify the interval at the letter A. __Per 5__   Circle if this interval is: (melodic) or harmonic.
   b) Identify the interval at the letter B. __min 3__   Circle if this interval is: (melodic) or harmonic.
   c) Identify the interval at the letter C. __Maj 2__   Circle if this interval is: (melodic) or harmonic.

2. The following is the opening theme from J.S. Bach's Menuet in E Major.

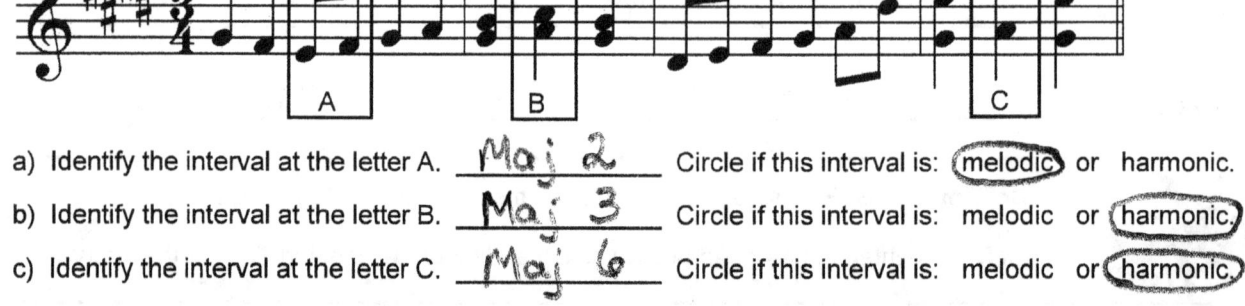

   a) Identify the interval at the letter A. __Maj 2__   Circle if this interval is: (melodic) or harmonic.
   b) Identify the interval at the letter B. __Maj 3__   Circle if this interval is: melodic or (harmonic).
   c) Identify the interval at the letter C. __Maj 6__   Circle if this interval is: melodic or (harmonic).

IDENTIFYING INTERVALS IN POLYPHONIC (TWO-PART) MUSIC

Polyphonic Texture: A multi-voiced texture that combines two or more equally important melodic lines. Polyphonic Music uses the techniques of Counterpoint (combining melodic lines into a single texture).

When two parts or voices on one staff move independently or use different rhythms, the upper (top) voice will use stems up and the lower (bottom) voice will use stems down. This is called **Double Stemming**. Intervals are written as both Melodic and Harmonic.

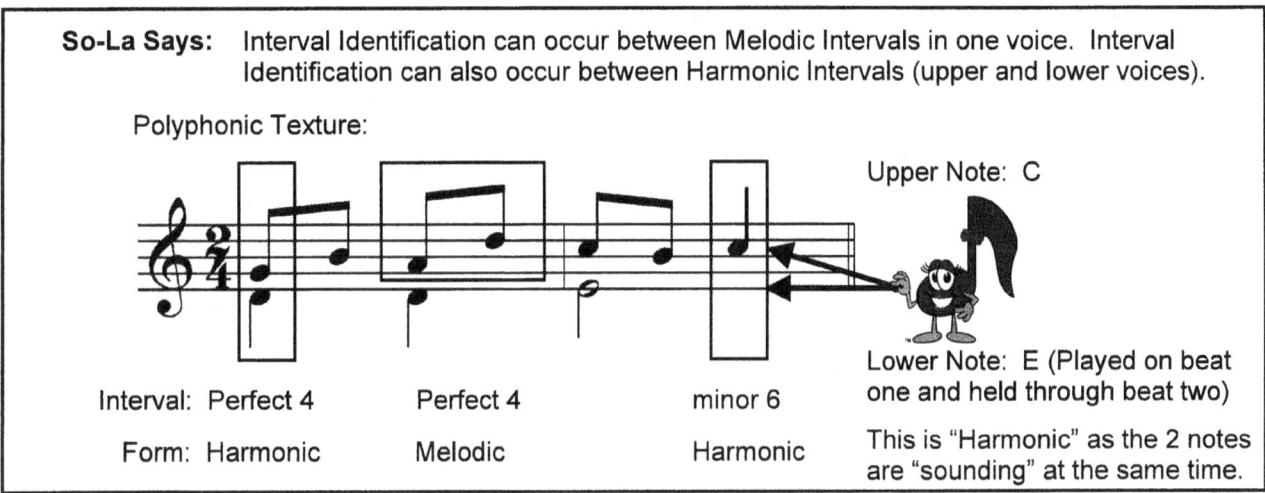

So-La Says: Interval Identification can occur between Melodic Intervals in one voice. Interval Identification can also occur between Harmonic Intervals (upper and lower voices).

Polyphonic Texture:

Upper Note: C
Lower Note: E (Played on beat one and held through beat two)
This is "Harmonic" as the 2 notes are "sounding" at the same time.

Interval: Perfect 4, Perfect 4, minor 6
Form: Harmonic, Melodic, Harmonic

♫ **Ti-Do Tip:** Observe whether the notes are in the Treble Staff or in the Bass Staff.

1. The following is a theme from Beethoven's Piano Sonata in D Major, Opus 10, No. 3.

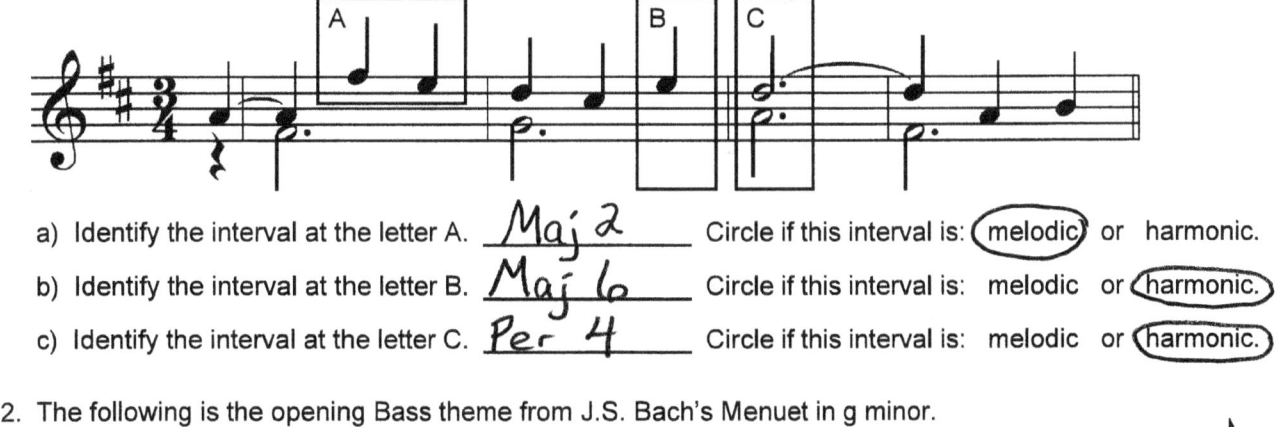

a) Identify the interval at the letter A. __Maj 2__   Circle if this interval is: (melodic) or harmonic.
b) Identify the interval at the letter B. __Maj 6__   Circle if this interval is: melodic or (harmonic).
c) Identify the interval at the letter C. __Per 4__   Circle if this interval is: melodic or (harmonic).

2. The following is the opening Bass theme from J.S. Bach's Menuet in g minor.

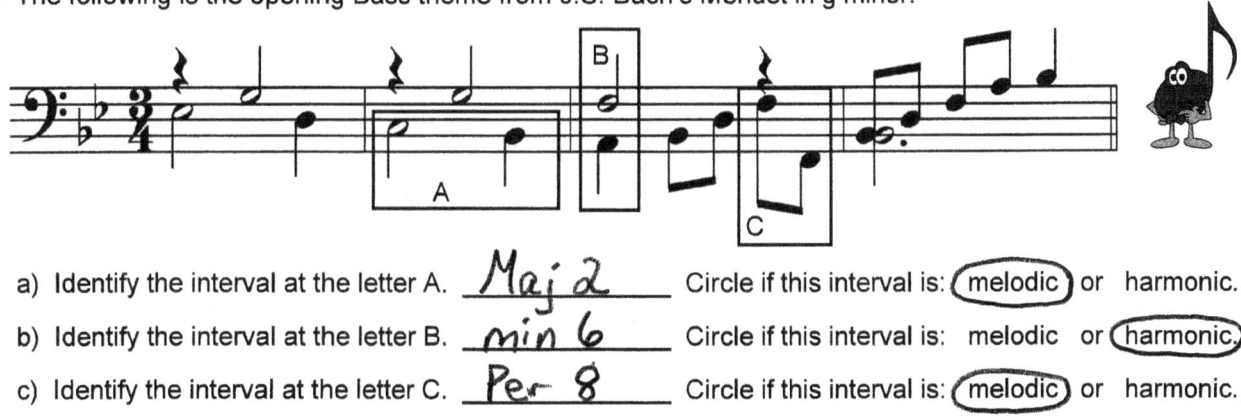

a) Identify the interval at the letter A. __Maj 2__   Circle if this interval is: (melodic) or harmonic.
b) Identify the interval at the letter B. __min 6__   Circle if this interval is: melodic or (harmonic).
c) Identify the interval at the letter C. __Per 8__   Circle if this interval is: (melodic) or harmonic.

PARALLEL and CONTRARY

The term "**Parallel**" refers to movement of 2 or more voices in the same direction (both voices ascending or both voices descending) while also maintaining the same numerical (interval number) distance. The type/quality of the intervals may change, but the interval numbers will stay the same.

The term "**Contrary**" refers to movement of 2 or more voices in the opposite direction (one voice ascending and one voice descending).

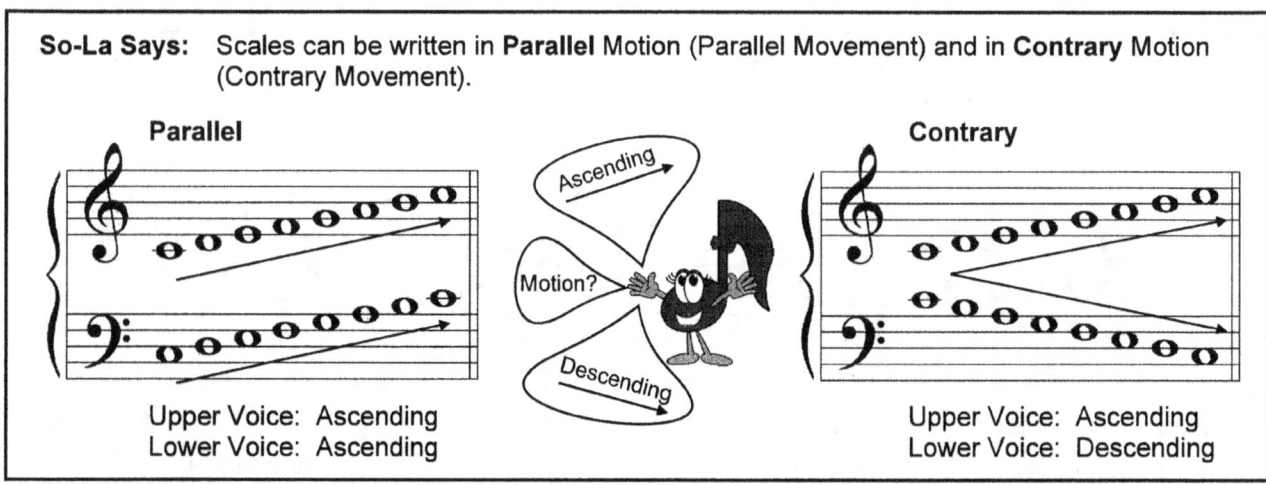

1. Fill in the blanks. Use the term ascending or the term descending.

    a) In Parallel Motion: Upper Voice - ascending, Lower Voice - __ascending__.

    b) In Parallel Motion: Upper Voice - descending, Lower Voice - __descending__.

    c) In Contrary Motion: Upper Voice - ascending, Lower Voice - __descending__.

    d) In Contrary Motion: Upper Voice - descending, Lower Voice - __ascending__.

The term "**Parallel**" is also used to describe the motion of intervals. A **Parallel Interval** is the movement of two voices in the same direction, keeping the same distance (interval) apart. The quality may be different.

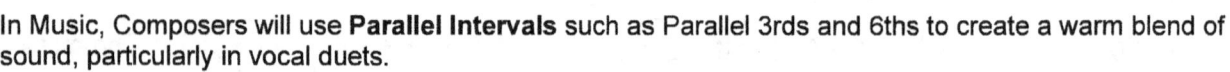

1. The following is the opening theme from J.S. Bach's Menuet in E Major.

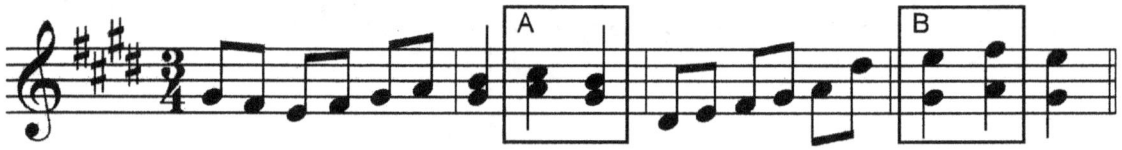

   a) Circle if the intervals at the letter A are: (**Parallel 3rds**) or Parallel 6ths or Parallel 8ths.

   b) Circle if the intervals at the letter B are: Parallel 3rds or (**Parallel 6ths**) or Parallel 8ths.

CHROMATIC & DIATONIC HALF STEPS, WHOLE STEPS and ENHARMONIC EQUIVALENTS

The "**Letter Name**" of a note (also called the "**Spelling**" of a note) refers to the specific name given to a note to identify the pitch.

Using accidentals (sharps and flats), each Black Key and four White Keys can be written using different letter names.

Composers will use the letter name of a note based upon the Key of the piece, the texture of the music, the melodic direction of the pitch and the harmonic patterns.

Enharmonic Equivalent: The same key on the keyboard (the same pitch) written using a different letter name.

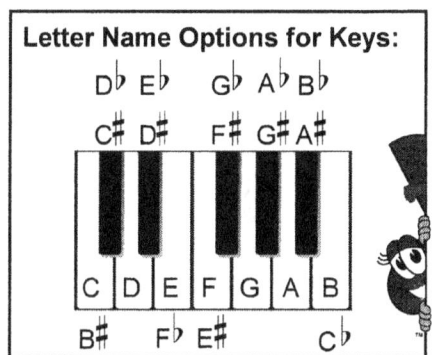

1. Write the Enharmonic Equivalent for the note in each measure. Name both notes.

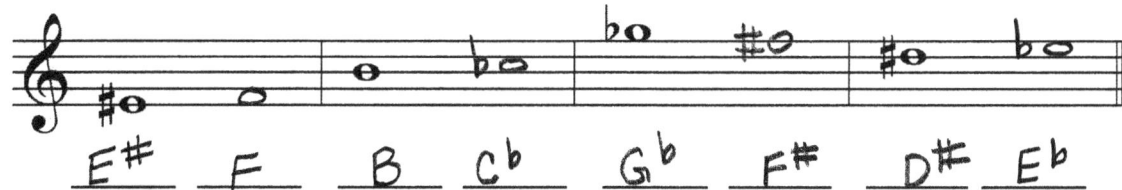

E#   F   B   Cb   Gb   F#   D#   Eb

So-La Says: Intervals of a 1st and a 2nd can be also be identified as **Half Steps** and **Whole Steps**.

Half Step: The distance from one note to the next note, above or below, black or white, no key in between. A Half Step can be written using the same letter name or using a different letter name.

Chromatic Half Step: A Half Step written using the same letter name. (F, F#)

Diatonic Half Step: A Half Step written using a different (neighboring, next door) letter name. (F, Gb)

Whole Step: The distance from one note to another with one key (black or white) in between. A Whole Step is written using a different (neighboring, next door) letter name. (F, G)

♫ **Ti-Do Tip:** A Half Step is also called a Semitone. A Whole Step is also called a Whole Tone or Tone.

2. Name each of the following as: DH (Diatonic Half Step), CH (Chromatic Half Step)
   WS (Whole Step)   or   EE (Enharmonic Equivalent).

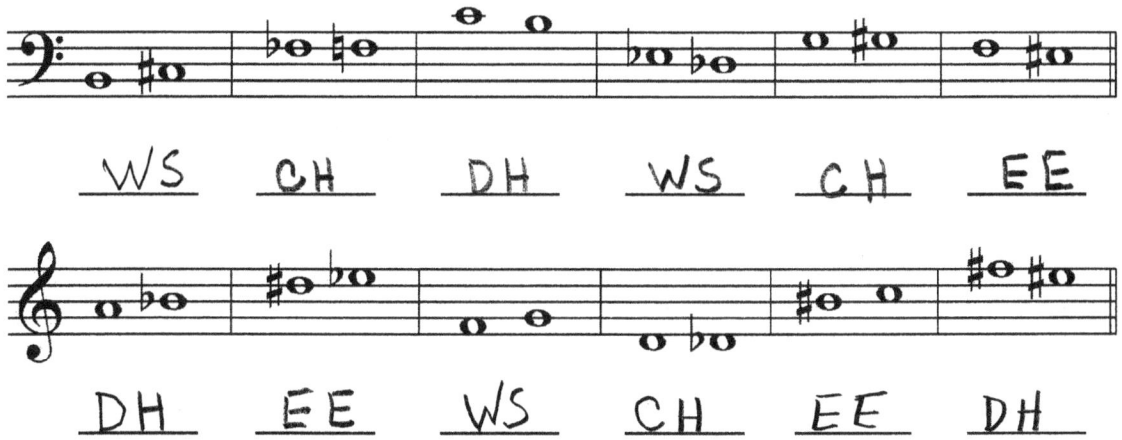

WS   CH   DH   WS   CH   EE

DH   EE   WS   CH   EE   DH

PARALLEL TRIADS

A **Triad** is written with 3 notes (Tri = Three). The notes of a Triad are the Root, the Third and the Fifth.

A **Major triad** is written with a Root + Major Third + Perfect Fifth.
A **minor triad** is written with a Root + minor Third + Perfect Fifth.

Parallel Triads (Parallel Major and minor triads) are Major and minor triads that share the same Root note.

So-La Says: The difference between a Major triad and a minor triad is the **type/quality of the third**. Major triad = Major third; minor triad = minor third.

Accidentals can be canceled by a **Bar Line** or by another **accidental**.

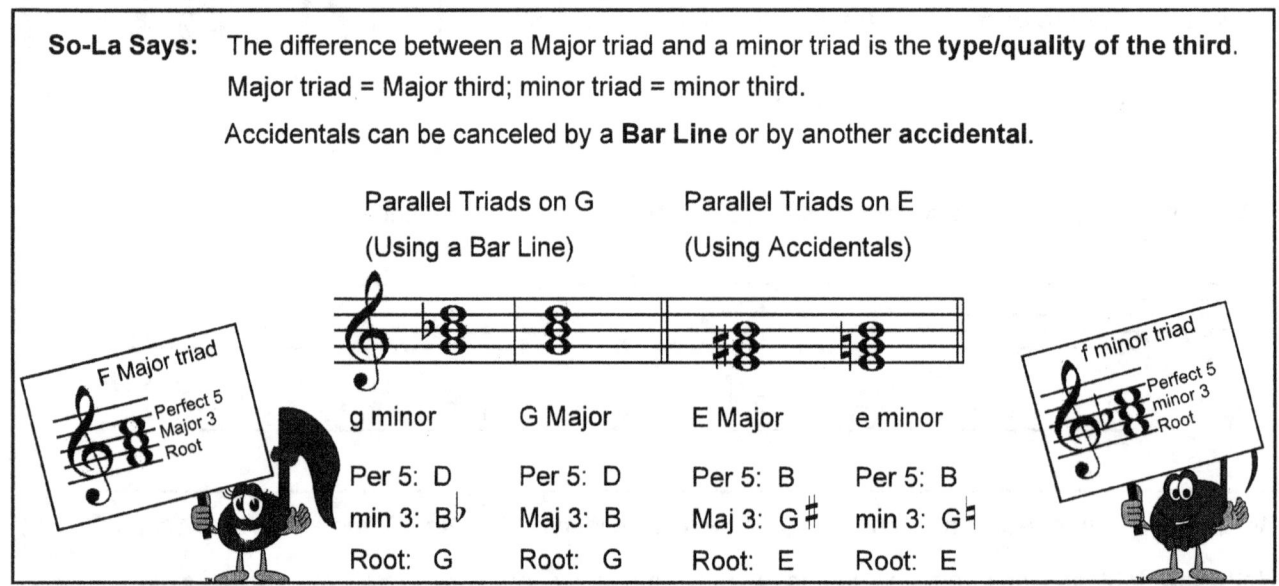

♫ **Ti-Do Tip:** To change a Major triad into a minor triad, lower the third a chromatic half step (semitone). To change a minor triad into a Major triad, raise the third a chromatic half step (semitone).

1. Following the example, change the Major triad into a minor triad or change the minor triad into a Major triad. Use accidentals. Name each triad.

Triad: __E__ Major __e__ minor __f__ minor __F__ Major __A__ Major __a__ minor

2. Identify the given triad as Major or minor. Write the Parallel minor triad for each Major triad or the Parallel Major triad for each minor triad. Use whole notes. Use accidentals when necessary.

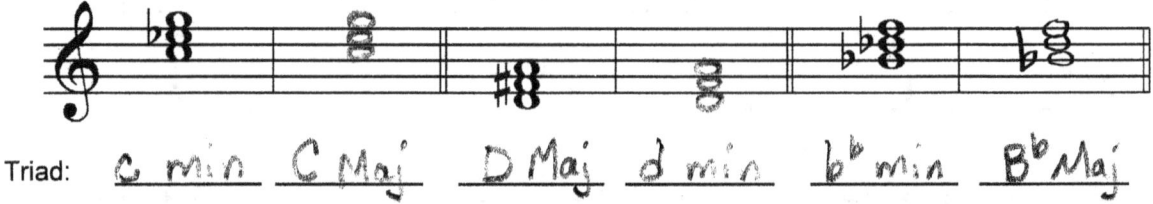

Triad: c min   C Maj   D Maj   d min   b♭ min   B♭ Maj

♫ **Ti-Do Time:** Your teacher will play a solid/blocked triad. Identify the type/quality as Major or minor.

Your teacher will then play a single note from the triad. Identify it as the root, the third or the fifth.

PRIMARY TRIADS, ROOT/QUALITY CHORD SYMBOLS and FUNCTIONAL CHORD SYMBOLS

Chords can be symbolized using **Root/Quality Chord Symbols** and using **Functional Chord Symbols**.

Root/Quality Chord Symbols are written above a Solid Triad and above the first note of a Broken Triad.
Functional Chord Symbols are written below a Solid Triad and below the first note of a Broken Triad.

So-La Says: Be sure that you have completed the Level 4 Supplemental Workbook!

Root/Quality Chord Symbols use letters to indicate the Root and the Quality of the Triad.

Major Triad = Root of the Triad, written using an upper case letter. (F)
Minor Triad = Root of the Triad, written using an upper case letter with an "m" for minor. (Fm)

Functional Chord Symbols use Roman Numerals to show the scale degree on which the triad is built and the type or quality (Major or minor) of the triad.

Major Triad = upper case Roman Numeral. (IV)
Minor Triad = lower case Roman Numeral. (iv)

Triads can be built on any note of a scale. **Primary Triads** are the triads built on the **Tonic**, the **Subdominant** and the **Dominant** Notes of the Major or (harmonic) minor scales.

♪ **Ti-Do Tip:**   Major Scale: I = Tonic Triad (Major)   Minor Scale: i = Tonic Triad (minor)
                              IV = Subdominant Triad (Major)   iv = Subdominant Triad (minor)
                              V = Dominant Triad (Major)   V = Dominant Triad (Major)

1. a) Name the Major or minor key.
   b) Write the Root/Quality Chord Symbol (C, Cm, F, Fm, G, etc.) above each triad.
   c) Write the Functional Chord Symbol (I, i, IV, iv, V) below each triad.

UltimateMusicTheory.com © Copyright 2017 Gloryland Publishing. All Rights Reserved.

IDENTIFYING ROOT POSITION, FIRST INVERSION and SECOND INVERSION TRIADS

A Triad is written with 3 notes (Tri = Three). The notes of a Triad are the Root, the Third and the Fifth.

An **Inversion** of a triad occurs when the Root of the triad is moved so that it is no longer the lowest note. A root position triad is all LINES or all SPACES. The Root of a root position triad is the lowest note.

So-La Says: In **any Inversion**, the triad position is always determined by the lowest note.

F Major triad: root position and inversions

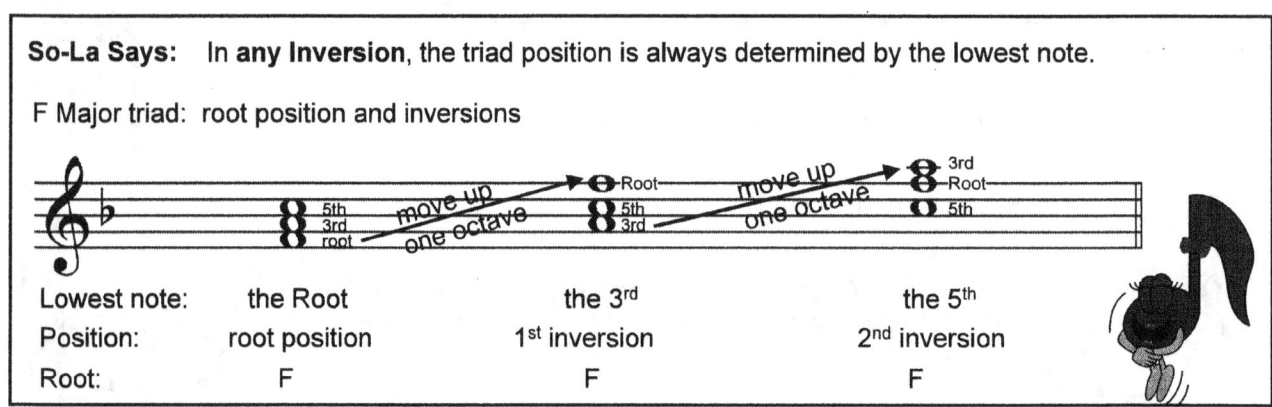

Lowest note:	the Root	the 3rd	the 5th
Position:	root position	1st inversion	2nd inversion
Root:	F	F	F

♪ **Ti-Do Tip:** The name of the Root of the triad remains the same in root position, 1st inv. and 2nd inv.

1. For each triad:
   a) Name the lowest note as the Root, the 3rd or the 5th.
   b) Identify the triad position as root pos (root position), 1st inv (1st inversion) or 2nd inv (2nd inversion).
   c) Identify the letter name of the Root note for each triad.

Key: B♭ Major   Key: c♯ minor

Lowest note:	the root	the 3rd	the 5th	the root	the 3rd	the 5th
Position:	root pos	1st inv	2nd inv	root pos	1st inv	2nd inv
Root:	B♭	B♭	B♭	C♯	C♯	C♯

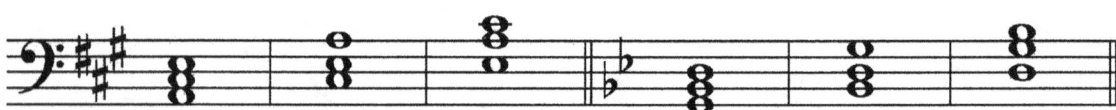

Key: A Major   Key: g minor

Lowest note:	the root	the 3rd	the 5th	the root	the 3rd	the 5th
Position:	root pos	1st inv	2nd inv	root pos	1st inv	2nd inv
Root:	A	A	A	G	G	G

♪ **Ti-Do Time:** LISTEN as your Teacher plays the triads on Page 34.

Identify if the triad played is solid or broken. Identify if it is in root position or an inversion.

WRITING ROOT POSITION, FIRST INVERSION and SECOND INVERSION TRIADS

The 3 notes of a triad can be arranged in any order. The lowest (bottom) note names the position.

Root Position (root pos) Triad = The Root is the lowest note (the bottom note of the triad).

First Inversion (1st inv) Triad = The Third is the lowest note (the bottom note of the triad).

Second Inversion (2nd inv) Triad = The Fifth is the lowest note (the bottom note of the triad).

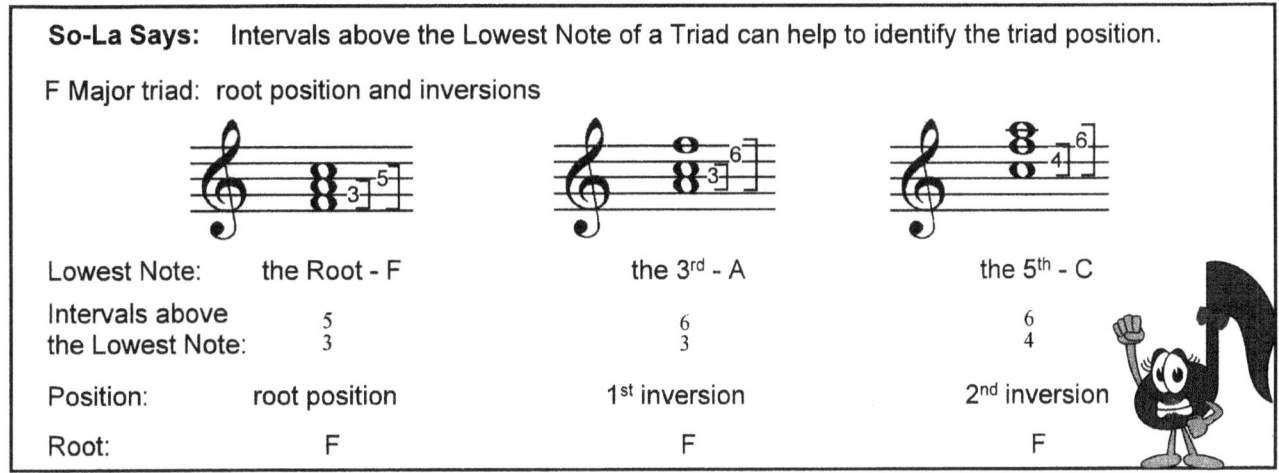

Triads can be written using a Key Signature or using accidentals.

1. Following the example, name the root position Major triad. Write the 1st inversion and 2nd inversion triads. Use whole notes. Use accidentals.

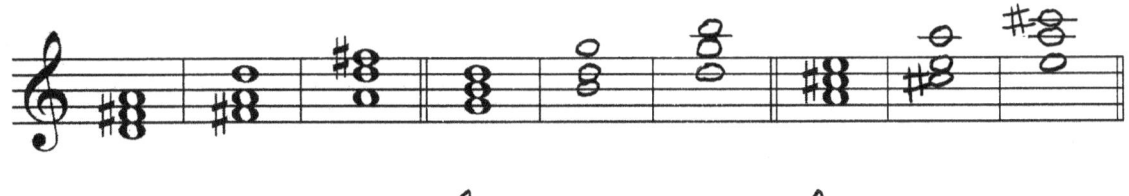

Triad: __D__ Major   __G__ Major   __A__ Major

♩ **Ti-Do Tip:** When writing triads using accidentals, observe the rules for Proper Placement of Accidentals.

Proper placement of 2 accidentals in triads and inversions:
1st accidental - written closer to the top note;
2nd accidental - written further away from the bottom note.

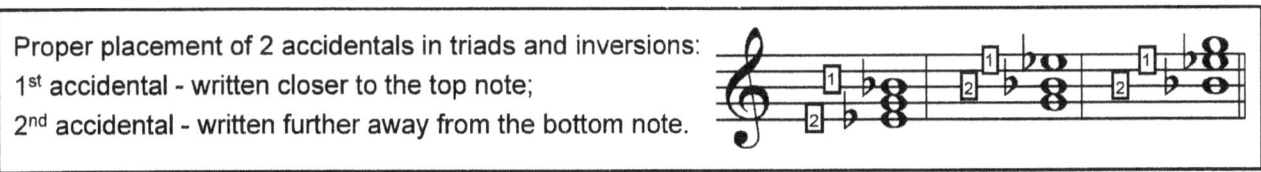

2. Following the example, name the root position minor triad. Write the 1st inversion and 2nd inversion triads. Use whole notes. Use accidentals.

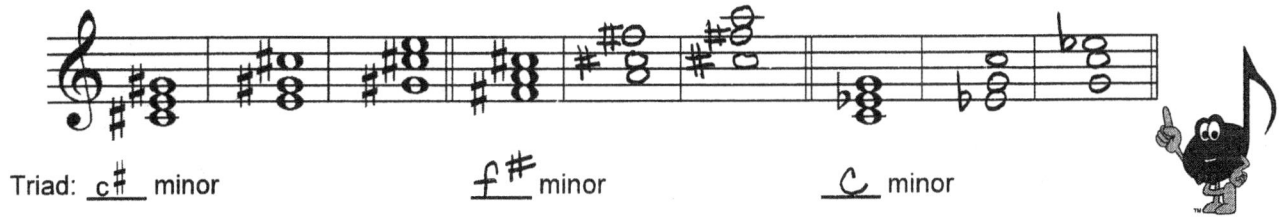

Triad: __c#__ minor   __f#__ minor   __C__ minor

CHORD SYMBOLS

Primary Triads are the triads built on the Tonic, Subdominant and Dominant notes.

Roman Numerals indicate the scale degree of the root note and the triad type/quality (Major or minor).

    Major Scale: I = Tonic Triad (Major)   Harmonic Minor Scale: i = Tonic Triad (minor)
                   IV = Subdominant Triad (Major)   iv = Subdominant Triad (minor)
                     V = Dominant Triad (Major)   V = Dominant Triad (Major)

Figured Bass Numbers are Arabic Numbers called "figures" which show the position of the chord (triad) by identifying the **intervals** (counting the number of letter names) above the bottom (lower) note.

    $\frac{5}{3}$ = Root Position $\frac{6}{3}$ = First Inversion $\frac{6}{4}$ = Second Inversion
      (root pos)   (1st inv)   (2nd inv)

The **Functional Chord Symbol** is the combination of the Roman Numeral Chord Symbols and the Figured Bass. It shows the Scale Degree of the Root, the Type/Quality of the Chord and the Position.

> **So-La Says:** Use the information in the Functional Chord Symbol to identify the Major or minor key.
>
>
>
> Functional Chord Symbol: $i\frac{5}{3}$ $IV\frac{6}{3}$ $V\frac{6}{4}$
>
> Root: C♯   Root: A   Root: G♯
> Degree: Tonic   Degree: Subdominant   Degree: Dominant
> Type/Quality: minor   Type/Quality: Major   Type/Quality: Major
> Position: Root Position   Position: 1st Inversion   Position: 2nd Inversion
> Key: c♯ minor   Key: E Major   Key: c♯ minor

1. For each of the following triads:
   a) Name the Root note.
   b) Identify the Degree as Tonic, Subdominant or Dominant.
   c) Identify the Type/Quality of the Triad as Major or minor.
   d) Name the position of the triad as root pos, 1st inv or 2nd inv.
   e) Name the Major or minor key.

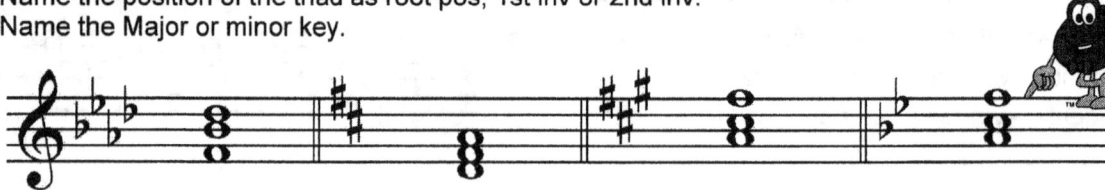

Functional Chord Symbol:	$iv\frac{6}{4}$	$I\frac{5}{3}$	$i\frac{6}{3}$	$V\frac{6}{3}$
Root:	B♭	D	F♯	F
Degree:	subdominant	Tonic	Tonic	Dominant
Type/Quality:	minor	Major	minor	Major
Position:	2nd inv	root pos	1st inv	1st inv
Key:	f minor	D Major	f♯ minor	B♭ Major

CHORD SYMBOL IDENTIFICATION

In a **Major key**, the Primary Triads are written using the notes of the Major scale. These triads are all Major.

In a **minor key**, the Primary Triads are written using the notes of the harmonic minor scale. The Tonic and Subdominant Triads are minor. The raised Leading Tone (raised 7th) creates the Major Dominant Triad.

So-La Says: The **traditional** (old-fashioned) method of identification for a Root Position Functional Chord Symbol was to use the "$^5_3$" Figured Bass numbers after the Roman Numeral.

The **preferred** (new, common) method of identification for a Root Position Functional Chord Symbol is to omit the Figured Bass and simply use the Roman Numeral.

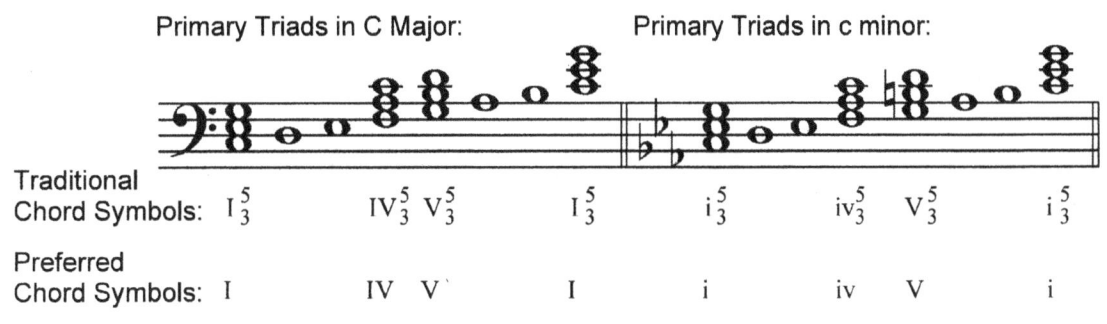

Primary Triads in C Major: Primary Triads in c minor:

Traditional Chord Symbols: I^5_3 IV^5_3 V^5_3 I^5_3 i^5_3 iv^5_3 V^5_3 i^5_3

Preferred Chord Symbols: I   IV   V   I   i   iv   V   i

♫ **Ti-Do Tip:** Upper Case Roman Numeral: Major triad; Lower Case Roman Numeral: minor triad.

The Functional Chord Symbol for a Tonic Major triad can be identified as I^5_3 or I.

The Functional Chord Symbol for a Tonic minor triad can be identified as i^5_3 or i.

1. The following Primary Triads are in the key of c minor. For each triad:
   a) Name the Root note.
   b) Identify the Degree as Tonic, Subdominant or Dominant.
   c) Name the position of the triad as root pos, 1st inv or 2nd inv.
   d) Write the Functional Chord Symbol (including Figured Bass for inversions) directly below each triad.

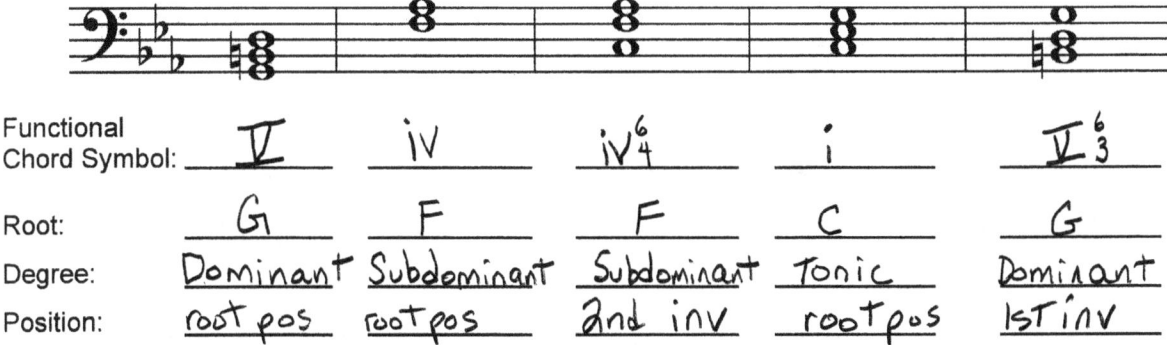

Functional Chord Symbol:	V	iV	iv$^6_4$	i	V$^6_3$
Root:	G	F	F	C	G
Degree:	Dominant	Subdominant	Subdominant	Tonic	Dominant
Position:	root pos	root pos	2nd inv	root pos	1st inv

 ♫ **Ti-Do Time:** LISTEN as your Teacher plays the triads on Pages 36 and 37.

Identify the position of the triad (root position, first inversion or second inversion).

Identify the type or quality of the triad (Major or minor).

TRIADS and KEY SIGNATURE IDENTIFICATION

A Key Signature can belong to a Major key or a minor key. To identify the key to which a triad belongs:

Step #1: Name the root note of the triad. Name the Major and the relative minor key for the Key Signature.

Step #2: Identify the names of the Primary Scale Degree Notes (the Tonic, Subdominant and Dominant) for both the Major and the relative minor keys of the Key Signature. This creates a **Key Identification Chart**. The Scale Degree Note that matches the root note of the triad will identify the Key that the triad belongs to.

Step #3: Name the key for the given triad and write the Functional Chord Symbol.

So-La Says: To identify the Functional Chord Symbol for the triad, observe the Key Signature and follow the steps to create a **Key Identification Chart**:

Step #1: Root note of triad; Major and relative minor keys:

Step #2: Primary Triad Major and minor Key Identification Chart:

Step #3: Name the key and the Functional Chord Symbol:

Root note: F

Major key: E♭ Major

minor key: c minor

Major key: E♭ Major
I = E♭ IV = A♭ V = B♭

minor key: c minor
i = C   iv = F   V = G

Key: c minor

Functional Chord Symbol: iv

♪ Ti-Do Tip: When writing triads using a Key Signature, the only triad that will be written with an accidental is the **Dominant triad** of the minor key. (Harmonic minor scale = raised 7th.)

1. For each triad:
   a) Name the root note. Observing the Key Signature, name the Major and relative minor keys.
   b) Complete the Key Identification Chart by naming the Primary Triad scale degree notes.
   c) Identify the Key and the Functional Chord Symbol.

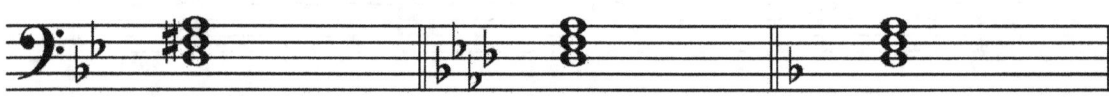

Root Note: D
Major key: B♭ Major
I = B♭ IV = E♭ V = F
minor key: g minor
i = G   iv = C   V = D
Triad key: g minor
Functional Chord Symbol: V

Root Note: D♭
Major key: A♭ Major
I = A♭ IV = D♭ V = E♭
minor key: f minor
i = F   iv = B♭ V = C
Triad key: A♭ Major
Functional Chord Symbol: IV

Root Note: D
Major key: F Major
I = F   IV = B♭ V = C
minor key: d minor
i = D   iv = G   V = A
Triad key: d minor
Functional Chord Symbol: i

BROKEN TRIADS in ROOT POSITION and INVERSIONS USING KEY SIGNATURES

A triad in **Close Position** is written as close together as possible. No interval is larger than a 6th.

A triad in close position is written as solid (blocked) or broken (ascending or descending), and in root position or an inversion.

To quickly identify the position/inversion of a triad (solid or broken), write the triad in root position inside of [square brackets]. The position of a triad is always determined by the lowest note of the triad.

    Lowest note: Root = Root Position
    Lowest note: The Third = First Inversion
    Lowest note: The Fifth = Second Inversion

To identify the Root note, the Type/Quality of the triad, the Position of the triad and the Key:

Step #1: Write the triad in root position (Solid/Blocked) in [square brackets].

Step #2: Use an arrow to identify the lowest note of the given triad as being the Root, the Third or the Fifth. (The location of the lowest note will identify the Position of the given triad.)

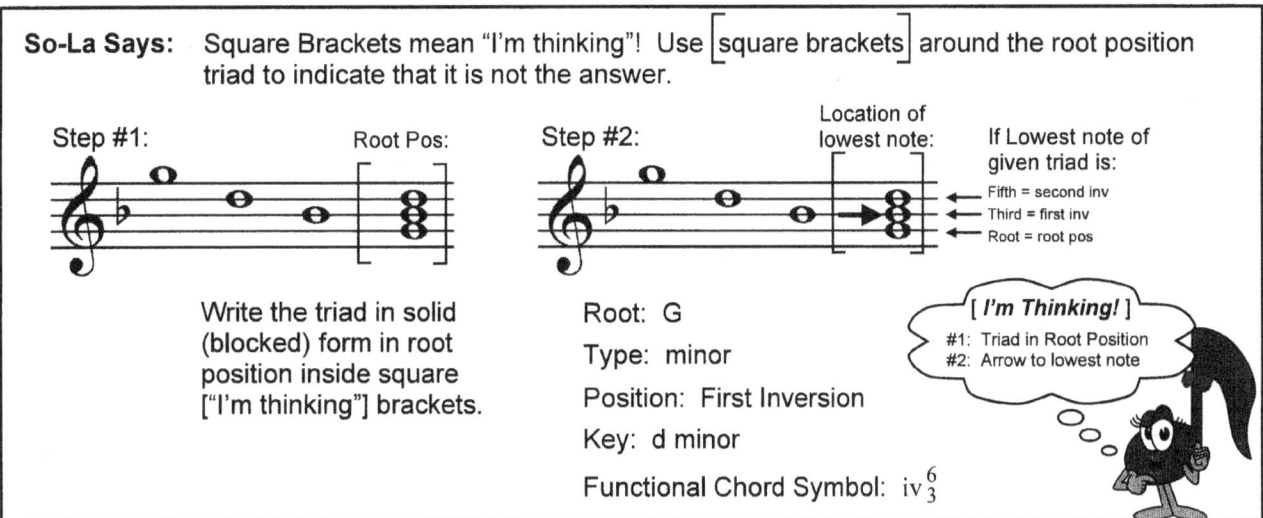

♫ **Ti-Do Tip:** The **Functional Chord Symbol** = Roman Numeral to indicate **Degree** and **Tonality** (I, i, IV, iv, V) plus Figured Bass Arabic numbers to indicate **Position/Inversion** ($\frac{5}{3}$, $\frac{6}{3}$, $\frac{6}{4}$).

1. For each triad:
   a) Inside the [square brackets], write the solid root position triad. Add an arrow to show the lowest note.
   b) Name the Root, the Type, the Position, the Major or minor Key and the Functional Chord Symbol.

Root: F   C   G#
Type: minor   Major   Major
Position: 2nd inv   1st inv   1st inv
Key: f minor   G Major   c# minor
Chord Symbol: i$\frac{6}{4}$ IV$\frac{6}{3}$ V$\frac{6}{3}$

ROOT/QUALITY CHORD SYMBOLS

Root/Quality Chord Symbols are Letter Names that indicate the quality (Major or minor) of a triad.

An upper case letter indicates a Major triad. (D = D Major triad)
An upper case letter with an "m" indicates a minor triad. (Dm = d minor triad)

  A Root/Quality Chord Symbol letter (or letter with an "m") = a Root Position Triad.

A **Slash Chord** is when the Root/Quality Chord Symbol indicates that another note other than the Root note is the lowest note of the triad.

  A Slash Chord is a Root/Quality Chord Symbol letter (or letter with an "m") followed by a **slash (/)** and another letter, indicating an inversion. The letter after the slash is the name of the lowest note of the triad.

> **So-La Says:** The Root/Quality Chord Symbol is a musical shorthand that indicates the Root note of the triad, the Quality (Major or minor) of the triad and the name of the lowest note.
>
> No "Slash" = the given note is the Root note of the triad.
> "Slash" (/) = the note written after the slash is the lowest note of the triad.

Root/Quality Chord Symbol "E" = E Major triad in root position.
Root/Quality Chord Symbol "Am/C" = a minor triad with C (the third) as the lowest note (1st inversion).
Root/Quality Chord Symbol "G/D" = G Major triad with D (the fifth) as the lowest note (2nd inversion).

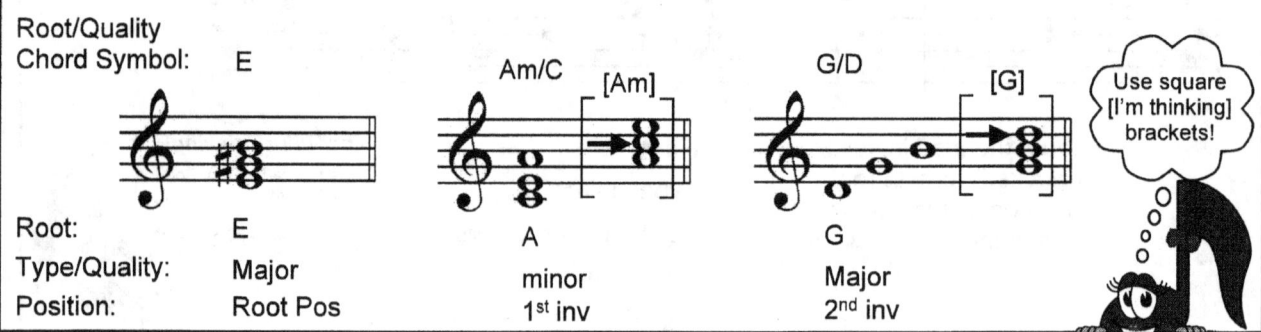

♫ **Ti-Do Tip:** The Root/Quality Slash Chord Symbol "C/E" is pronounced "C Slash E".

The Root/Quality Slash Chord Symbol "Cm/E♭" is pronounced "C minor Slash E flat".

1. The following triads are written using accidentals. Use square [I'm thinking] brackets to show your work.

    a) Below each triad, name the Root note, the Type/Quality (Major or minor) and the Position (root pos, 1st inv or 2nd inv).
    b) Above each triad, write the Root/Quality Chord Symbol.

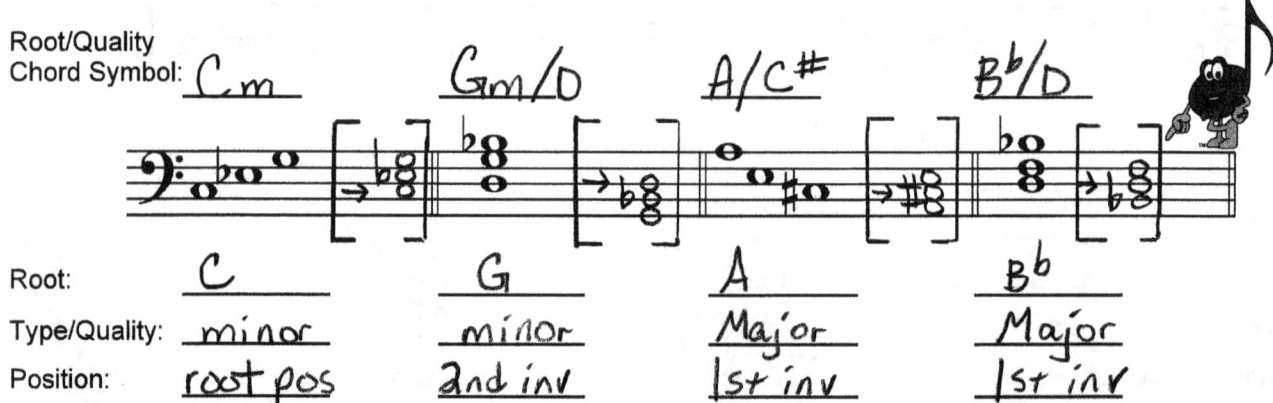

WRITING TRIADS, ROOT/QUALITY CHORD SYMBOLS and FUNCTIONAL CHORD SYMBOLS.

Root/Quality Chord Symbols identify the Root, the Quality and the lowest note (the Slash = an inversion). It is written above the triad.

Functional Chord Symbols identify the Root, the Quality and the Scale Degree. (The added Figured Bass indicates the Position of the triad.) It is written below the triad.

So-La Says: To write a specific Primary Triad using a Key Signature, follow these steps:

Write the solid/blocked Dominant triad of c minor in second inversion.

Step #1: Write the Key Signature.

Step #2: Write the Root Position Triad in square ["I'm thinking"] brackets at the end of the measure.

Step #3: Write the inversion. Write the Root/Quality Chord Symbol above and the Functional Chord Symbol below.

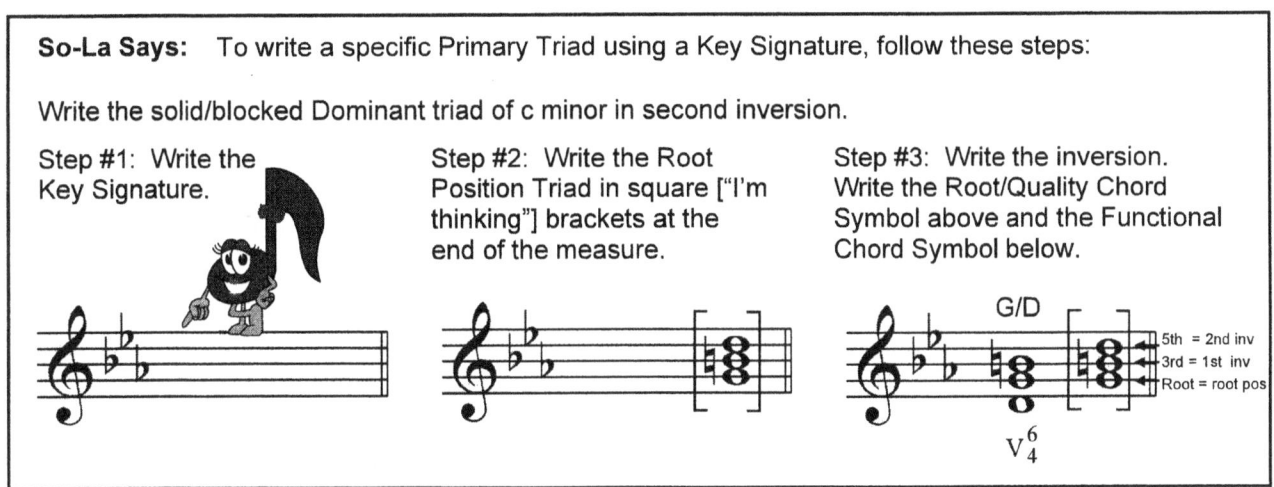

♪ **Ti-Do Tip:** If the root position triad in the square [I'm thinking] brackets is written with an accidental, the accidental **must be repeated** when writing the inversion of the triad.

1. Write the following solid/blocked triads. Use a Key Signature. Use whole notes. Write the root position triad in square ["I'm thinking] brackets (at end of measure). Write the triad in the inversion. Write the Root/Quality Chord Symbol above each triad. Write the Functional Chord Symbol below each triad.

   a) Tonic triad of D Major, second inversion
   b) Subdominant triad of E flat Major, first inversion
   c) Dominant triad of f minor, second inversion
   d) Subdominant triad of b minor, first inversion

Root/Quality Chord Symbol: a) D/A   b) A♭/C   c) C/G   d) Em/G

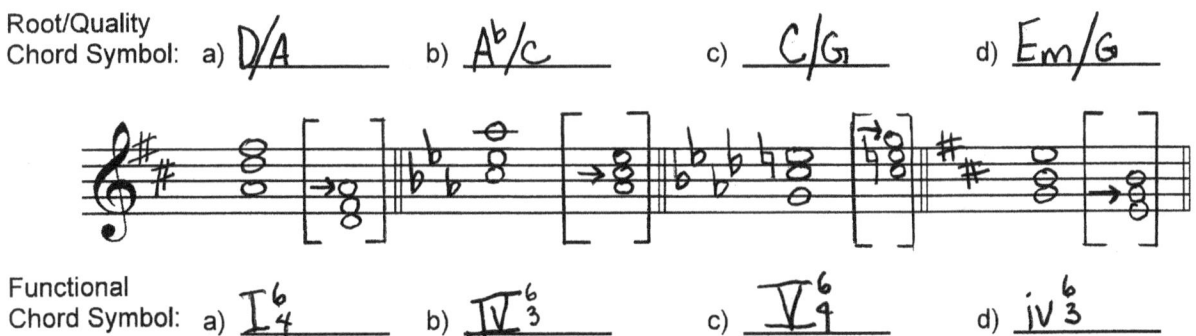

Functional Chord Symbol: a) I_4^6 b) IV_3^6 c) V_4^6 d) iv_3^6

♪ **Ti-Do Time:** LISTEN as your Teacher plays the triads on Pages 40 and 41.

Identify the position of the triad (root position, first inversion or second inversion).

Identify the type or quality of the triad (Major or minor).

DOMINANT SEVENTH CHORDS, MAJOR KEYS

A **Dominant Seventh Chord** is a 4-note chord with a Root (the Dominant), a Third, a Fifth and a Seventh.
A **Dominant 7th Chord** = Root - Major 3 - Perfect 5 - minor 7 (Major triad + minor 7 = Major-minor 7th Chord)

The Dominant 7th (Dom 7th) Chord (V7) is a Major-minor 7th Chord built on the fifth degree of the scale.

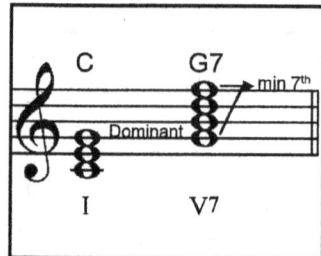

The **Root/Quality Chord Symbol** for a Dom 7th Chord in root position is the upper case letter name of the root note of the Dominant triad with a "7" beside it.

G7: G = Major triad with root note G; 7 = interval of a min 7th above the root note.

The **Functional Chord Symbol** for a Dom 7th Chord in root position is V7.
V7: V = Dominant triad; 7 = interval of a minor 7th above the Dominant note.

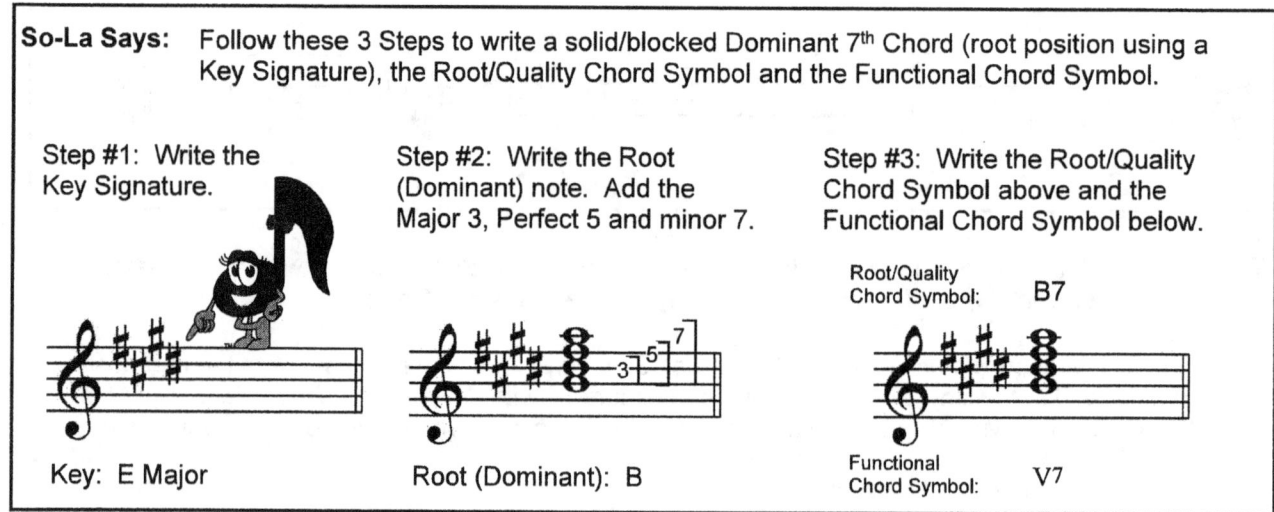

So-La Says: Follow these 3 Steps to write a solid/blocked Dominant 7th Chord (root position using a Key Signature), the Root/Quality Chord Symbol and the Functional Chord Symbol.

Step #1: Write the Key Signature.
Step #2: Write the Root (Dominant) note. Add the Major 3, Perfect 5 and minor 7.
Step #3: Write the Root/Quality Chord Symbol above and the Functional Chord Symbol below.

Key: E Major
Root (Dominant): B
Root/Quality Chord Symbol: B7
Functional Chord Symbol: V7

♪ **Ti-Do Tip:** In a Major key using a Key Signature, no additional accidentals are needed. The intervals above the Dominant are already the **Major 3**, the **Perfect 5** and the **minor 7**.

1. Write the following root position solid/blocked chords. Use a Key Signature. Use whole notes. Write the Root/Quality Chord Symbol above each chord. Write the Functional Chord Symbol below each chord.

    a) Dominant 7th Chord of D Major
    b) Dominant 7th Chord of E♭ Major
    c) Dominant 7th Chord of F Major
    d) Dominant 7th Chord of E Major

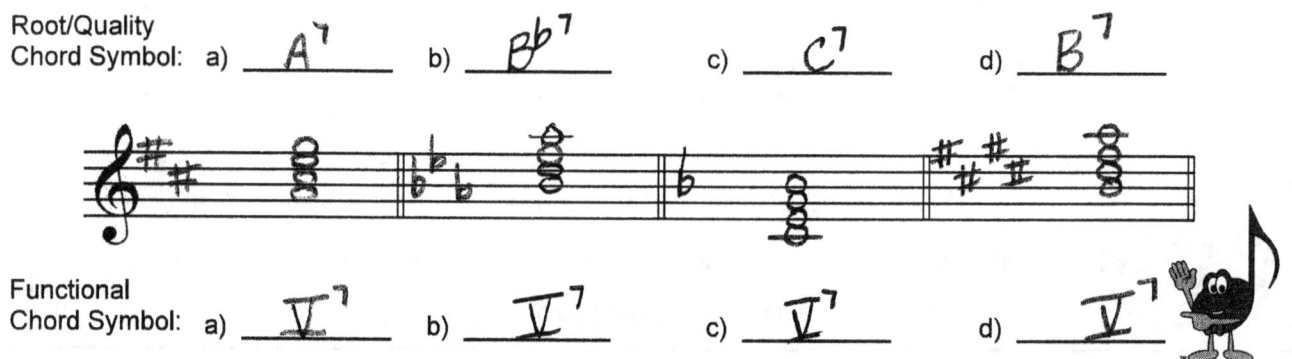

Root/Quality Chord Symbol: a) A7 b) B♭7 c) C7 d) B7

Functional Chord Symbol: a) V7 b) V7 c) V7 d) V7

DOMINANT SEVENTH CHORDS, MINOR KEYS

The Dominant 7th Chord (V7) is a Major-minor 7th Chord built on the fifth degree of the harmonic minor scale.
A **Dominant 7th Chord** = Root - Major 3 - Perfect 5 - minor 7 (Major triad + minor 7 = Major-minor 7th Chord)

To write the Dominant 7th Chord in a minor key, use the notes of the harmonic minor scale. An accidental will be needed on the (raised) Leading Tone.

In the Basic Rudiments Workbook, Scale Degrees and Harmonic Minor Scales are introduced in Lesson 6 and Dominant Triads are introduced in Lesson 7.

Complete the **Basic Workbook** and **UMT Level 4 Supplemental Workbook** before beginning the **UMT Level 5 Supplemental Workbook** so that you have a solid foundation in understanding the Dominant triad in Major and minor keys.

The raised 7th of the harmonic minor scale is the Leading Tone ($\hat{7}$). This is the 7th degree above the Tonic. The 7th of the Dominant 7th Chord is the interval of a 7th above the Dominant. This is the Subdominant ($\hat{4}$).

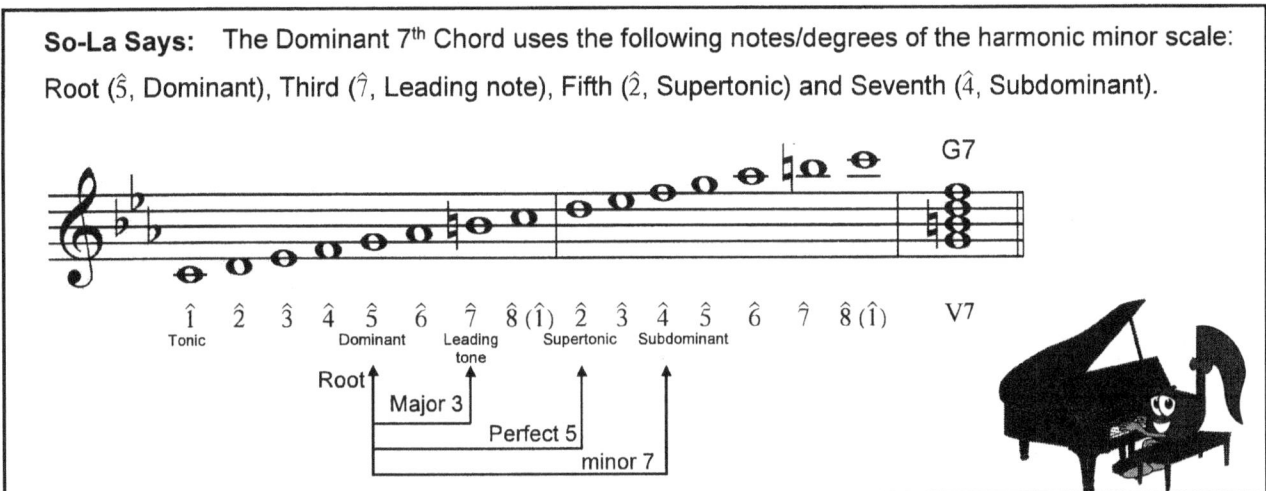

So-La Says: The Dominant 7th Chord uses the following notes/degrees of the harmonic minor scale: Root ($\hat{5}$, Dominant), Third ($\hat{7}$, Leading note), Fifth ($\hat{2}$, Supertonic) and Seventh ($\hat{4}$, Subdominant).

♪ **Ti-Do Tip:** In a minor key using a Key Signature, an accidental will be needed to raise the Leading Tone of the harmonic minor scale. This will create the Major 3 of the Dominant 7th chord.

1. Write the following root position solid/blocked chords. Use a Key Signature. Use whole notes. Write the Root/Quality Chord Symbol above each chord. Write the Functional Chord Symbol below each chord.

   a) Dominant 7th Chord of b minor
   b) Dominant 7th Chord of c minor
   c) Dominant 7th Chord of d minor
   d) Dominant 7th Chord of c♯ minor

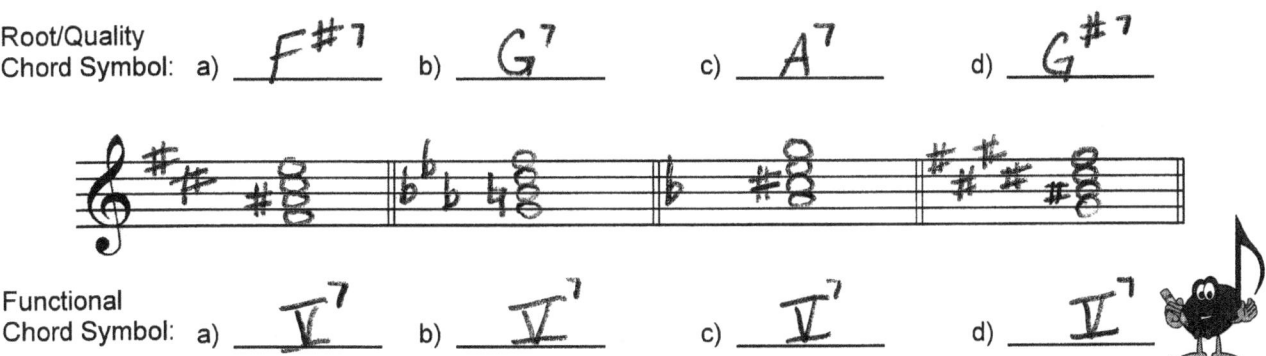

Root/Quality Chord Symbol: a) F♯7   b) G7   c) A7   d) G♯7

Functional Chord Symbol: a) V7   b) V7   c) V7   d) V7

TONIC MAJOR/TONIC MINOR DOMINANT SEVENTH CHORDS

Dominant 7th Chords can be written using a **Key Signature** or using **accidentals**.

Tonic Major and minor keys are Parallel Keys. They share the same Tonic note, but they have different Key Signatures. (Relative Major/minor keys have the same Key Signature.)

Tonic Major and minor keys have the same Dominant 7th Chord (their V7 Chords use the same notes).

When written using a Key Signature, the Dominant 7th Chord will belong to either the Major or the minor key. When written using accidentals, the Dominant 7th Chord will belong to both the Tonic Major and minor keys.

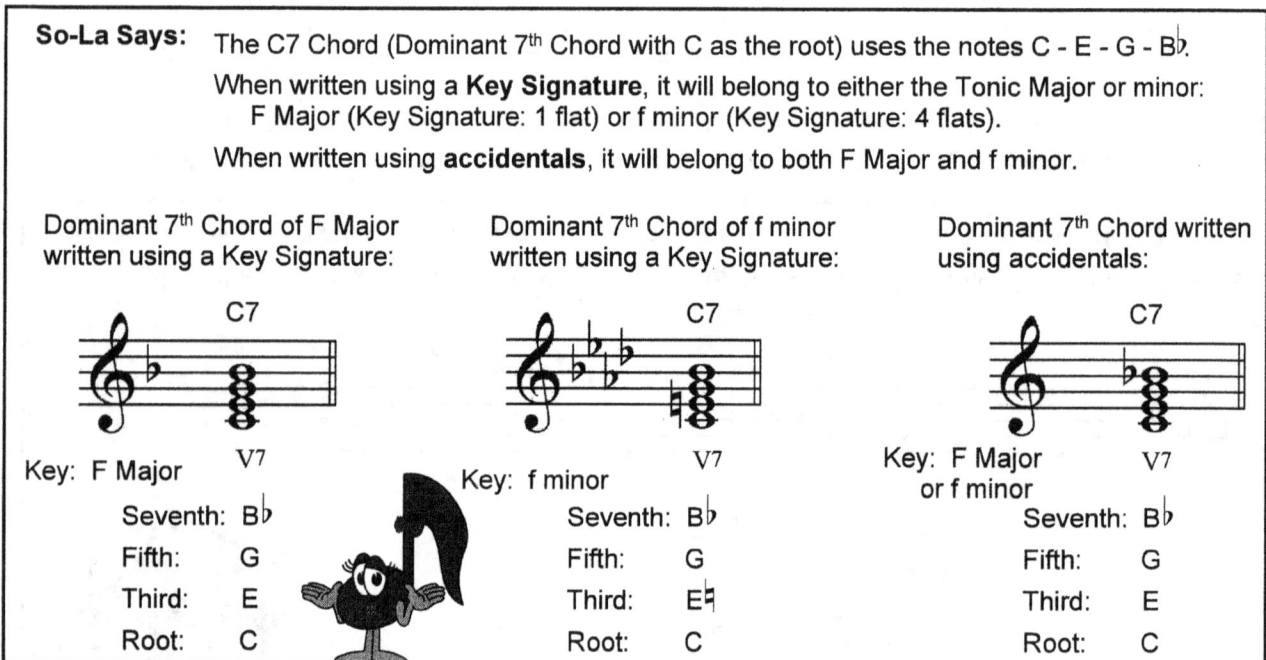

So-La Says: The C7 Chord (Dominant 7th Chord with C as the root) uses the notes C - E - G - B♭.
When written using a **Key Signature**, it will belong to either the Tonic Major or minor:
F Major (Key Signature: 1 flat) or f minor (Key Signature: 4 flats).
When written using **accidentals**, it will belong to both F Major and f minor.

Dominant 7th Chord of F Major written using a Key Signature:
Key: F Major, V7
Seventh: B♭
Fifth: G
Third: E
Root: C

Dominant 7th Chord of f minor written using a Key Signature:
Key: f minor, V7
Seventh: B♭
Fifth: G
Third: E♮
Root: C

Dominant 7th Chord written using accidentals:
Key: F Major or f minor, V7
Seventh: B♭
Fifth: G
Third: E
Root: C

♪ **Ti-Do Tip:** Natural signs are needed only to cancel an actual sharp or flat. If the sharp or flat does not appear in the measure, a natural sign is not needed to cancel it.

1. Following the examples, write the Dominant Seventh Chord in root position for each Tonic Major/minor key. Use accidentals. Use whole notes. Name the Root, Third, Fifth and Seventh notes.

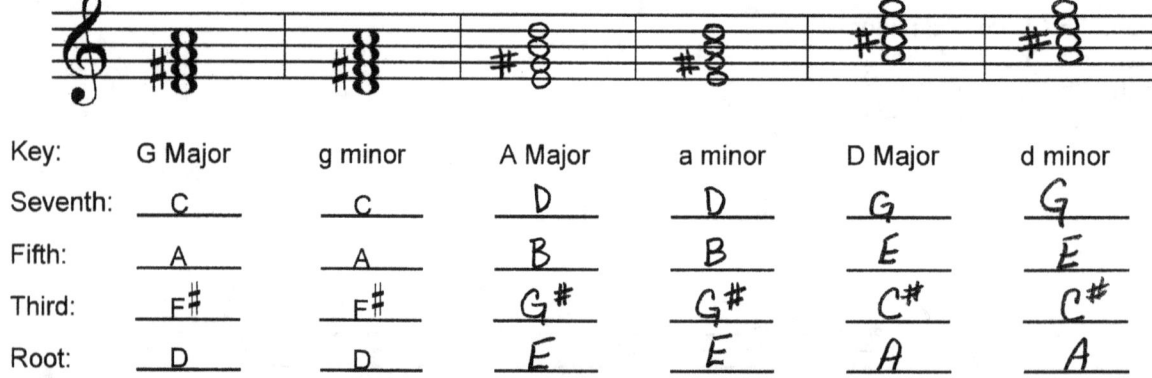

Key:	G Major	g minor	A Major	a minor	D Major	d minor
Seventh:	C	C	D	D	G	G
Fifth:	A	A	B	B	E	E
Third:	F♯	F♯	G♯	G♯	C♯	C♯
Root:	D	D	E	E	A	A

 ♪ **Ti-Do Time:** LISTEN as your Teacher plays the chords on Page 44.

Can you hear a difference between the Tonic Major and Tonic minor Dominant 7th Chords?

ACCIDENTAL PLACEMENT in DOMINANT SEVENTH CHORDS

Root position Dominant 7th Chords in **Close Position** are written with all notes as close together as possible. All 4 notes will be either on **4 lines** or in **4 spaces**. Each note is a 3rd apart.

Proper placement of 2 accidentals in chords:
1st accidental - written closer to the top note;
2nd accidental - written further away from the bottom note.

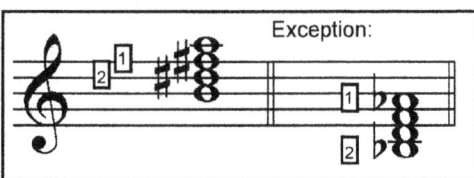

Exception for Proper Placement of 2 accidentals: When a chord contains two accidentals, and they are a seventh apart (top and bottom notes), the accidentals are placed in normal position close to the noteheads.

Proper placement of 3 accidentals in chords:
1st accidental - written closer to the top note;
2nd accidental - written further away from the bottom note;
3rd accidental - written furthest away from the middle note.

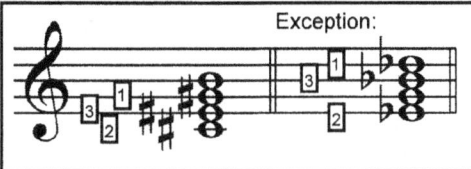

Exception for Proper Placement of 3 accidentals: When a chord contains three accidentals, and two notes with accidentals are a seventh apart, the accidentals are placed in normal position - closest to the top and bottom noteheads. The middle accidental is then written further away from the top and bottom notes.

So-La Says: The Dominant 7th Chord of c# minor is the only chord at this level with **4 accidentals**.

1st accidental - written closer to the top note;
2nd accidental - written closer to the bottom note;
3rd accidental - written further away from the 2nd highest note;
4th accidental - written furthest away from the 2nd lowest note.

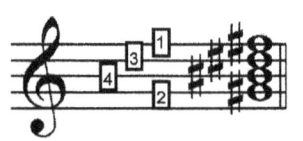

1. Write the Dominant 7th Chord in root position for each key. Use accidentals. Use whole notes. Write the Root/Quality Chord Symbol above each chord. Write the Functional Chord Symbol below each chord.

    a) Dominant 7th Chord of A♭ Major
    b) Dominant 7th Chord of E Major
    c) Dominant 7th Chord of f# minor
    d) Dominant 7th Chord of c# minor

Root/Quality
Chord Symbol: a)  b)  c) 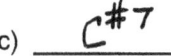 d)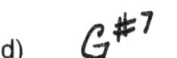

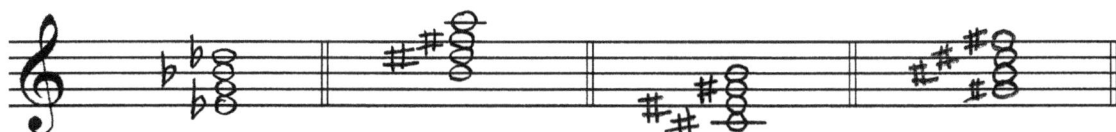

Functional
Chord Symbol: a) V^7 b) V^7 c) V^7 d) V^7

 ♪ **Ti-Do Time:** Your Teacher will play a solid (blocked) root position Dominant 7th Chord. Your teacher will then play one of the 4 notes. Identify the note as the Root, 3rd, 5th or 7th.

IDENTIFYING BROKEN TRIADS in CLOSE POSITION

A Triad or Chord in **Close Position** is written as close together as possible.

Solid (Blocked) form = notes are written one above the other, played at the same time (harmonic).

Broken form = notes are written one note after the other, played separately (melodic).
Broken form **direction** = notes can be written ascending, descending or in any order.

The **position** is always determined by the lowest note (the note written at the lowest pitch, no matter in what order it appears in the broken triad or chord).

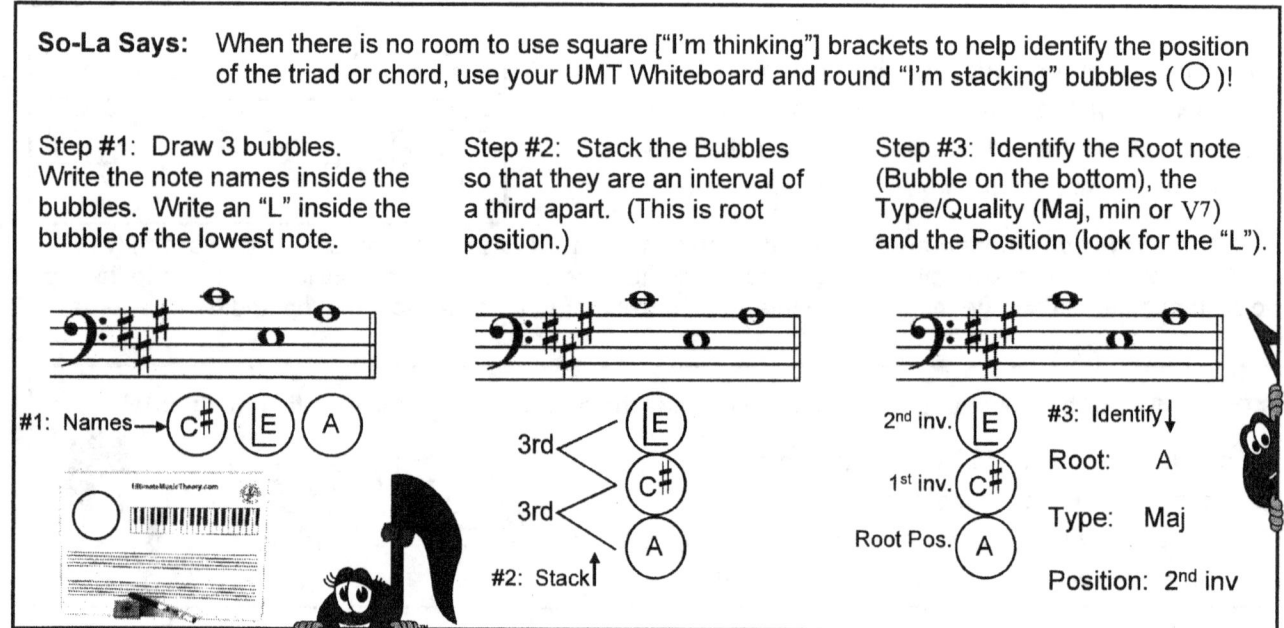

♪ **Ti-Do Tip:** To identify the Position, look for the "L": L in the Bottom (lowest) Bubble = Root Position
L in the Middle Bubble = First Inversion
L in the Top (highest) Bubble = Second Inversion

1. Identify the Root, Type/Quality and Position for each triad. Show your work one step at a time.

    a) Step #1: Write the letter names in the bubbles below each note. Identify the Lowest "L" Bubble.
    b) Step #2: Stack the bubbles in 3rd's to build a Root Position triad.
    c) Step #3: Identify the Root, the Type/Quality and the Position of each broken triad.

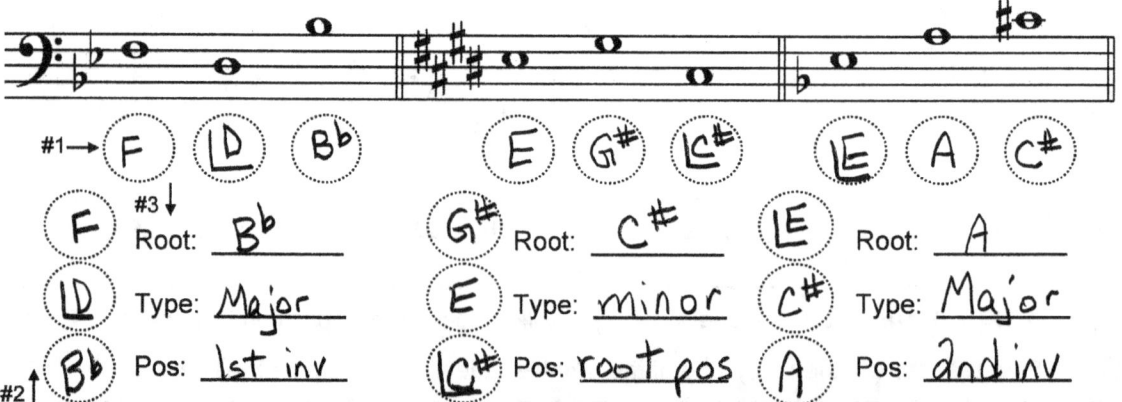

UltimateMusicTheory.com © Copyright 2017 Gloryland Publishing. All Rights Reserved. 46

IDENTIFYING BROKEN DOMINANT SEVENTH CHORDS in CLOSE POSITION

A **Triad** (3-note Chord) uses 3 different note names. A **Dominant 7th Chord** uses 4 different notes names.

The Root/Quality Chord Symbol is written above the first note of the broken Triad or Chord.
The Functional Chord Symbol is written below the first note of the broken Triad or Chord.

So-La Says: To identify the Root/Quality Chord Symbol and the Functional Chord Symbol, use the Whiteboard to identify the Root, Type/Quality, Position and Key Identification Chart.

Show your work: use square "I'm thinking" brackets or round "I'm stacking" bubbles.

Root/Quality Chord Symbol: G7

Functional Chord Symbol: V7

Root/Quality Chord Symbol: G7

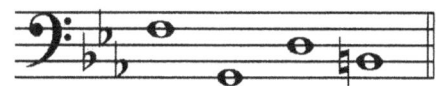

Functional Chord Symbol: V7

Key Identification Chart:

Major Key: E♭ Major
I = E♭   IV = A♭   V = B♭

minor key: c minor
i = C   iv = F   V = G

Root: G
Type: V7
Position: Root Pos.
Key: c minor

Root: G
Type: V7
Position: Root Pos.
Key: c minor

Use either UMT Learning Tool to get the Correct Answer!

♪ **Ti-Do Tip:** Show Your Work! Use your UMT Learning Tools and your Whiteboard to be successful!

1. Identify the Root/Quality Chord Symbols and Functional Chord Symbols. Show ALL your work!

Root/Quality Chord Symbol: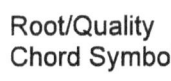

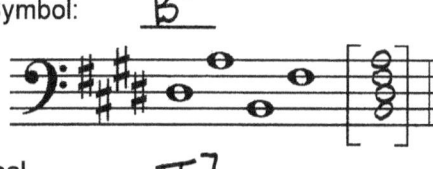

Functional Chord Symbol: V7

Root/Quality Chord Symbol: B7

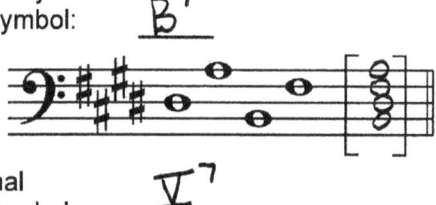

Functional Chord Symbol: V7

Key Identification Chart:

Major Key: E Major
I = E   IV = A   V = B

minor key: C# minor
i = C#   iv = F#   V = G#

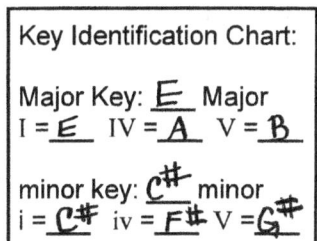

Root: B
Type: V7
Position: root pos
Key: E Major

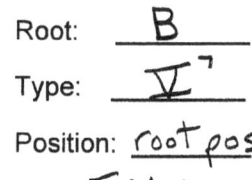

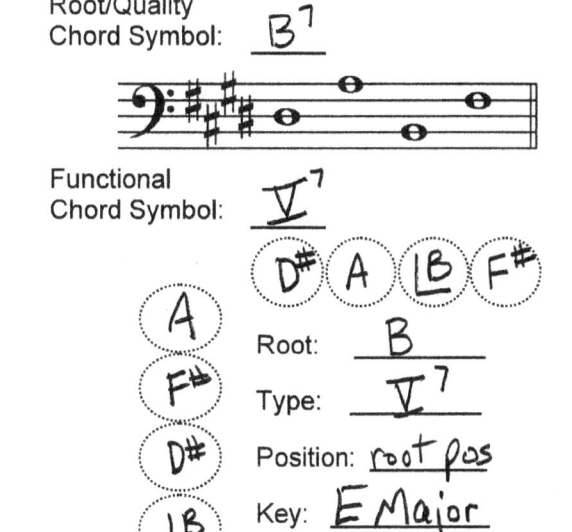

Root: B
Type: V7
Position: root pos
Key: E Major

WRITING TRIADS and DOMINANT SEVENTH CHORDS

When writing **Triads or Dominant Seventh Chords** using a Key Signature, the Key Signature is written only once at the beginning of the staff after the clef. The same Key Signature applies to all measures.

When writing triads or chords using a Key Signature, if the Key Signature changes for each measure, the new Key Signature is written at the beginning of each measure. The clef sign is not repeated.

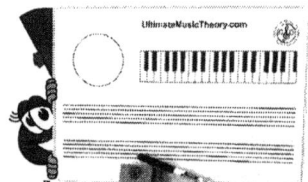

So-La Says: Understanding Root/Quality Chord Symbols makes playing popular music so much fun!

Be a Detective! Use the "clues" in the Root/Quality Chord Symbol and in the Functional Chord Symbol to write the Triad or Dominant Seventh Chord.

Use your **UMT Whiteboard** to write out any of the **UMT Learning Tools** needed to successfully complete each question.

1. Write the following solid (blocked) Triads or Chords in F Major. Use a Key Signature and accidentals if needed. Use whole notes.

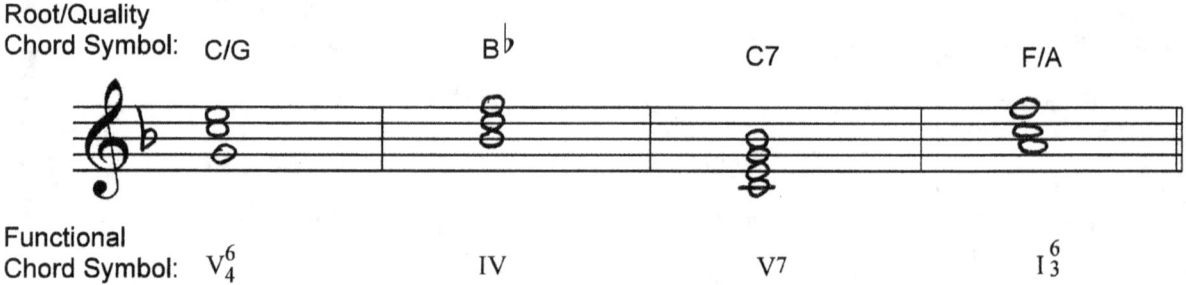

Root/Quality Chord Symbol: C/G, B♭, C7, F/A

Functional Chord Symbol: V^6_4, IV, V7, I^6_3

2. Write the Key Signature and the solid (blocked) Dominant 7th Chord for each of the following keys. Use accidentals if needed. Use whole notes. Write the Root/Quality Chord Symbol above each chord.

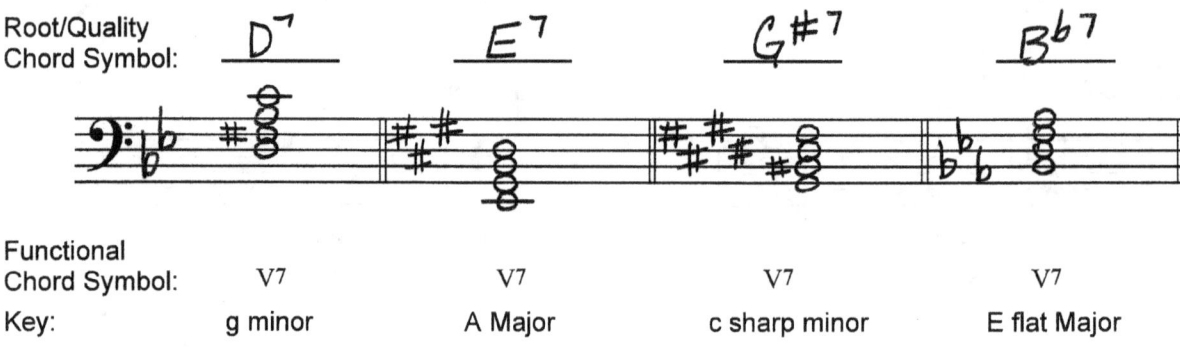

Root/Quality Chord Symbol: D^7, E^7, $G\sharp^7$, $B\flat^7$

Functional Chord Symbol: V7, V7, V7, V7

Key: g minor, A Major, c sharp minor, E flat Major

♪ **Ti-Do Time:** Play the triads and chords on Page 48 in solid (blocked) form.

Improvise! Play each triad and chord in broken form. Play ascending, descending or play the notes in any order. How many different ways can you play each triad/chord?

LISTEN as your Teacher plays the solid triads and chords on Page 48 in any order. Identify if your Teacher is playing a 3-note Triad or a 4-note Chord.

MUSICAL TERMS and SIGNS

Musical Terms and Signs indicate how the music should be played. The composer notates the music with: Articulation, Signs, Terms, Tempo, Changes in Tempo, Dynamics and Stylistic or Style in Performance.

Articulation - how a note is played *leggiero* - light, nimble, quick

Signs - symbols in the music 𝄋 - *dal segno, D. S.,* from the sign

Terms - written in the music *poco* - little
molto - much, very

Tempo - speed at which music is played *vivace* - lively, brisk

Changes in Tempo - speed *rubato* - some freedom of tempo to enhance musical expression

Dynamics - volume of sound *diminuendo, dim.* - becoming softer

Stylistic (Style) - emotion, mood *espressivo, espress.* - expressive, with expression
spiritoso - spirited
tranquillo - quiet, tranquil

Musical Terms and Signs for string instruments indicate specific performance details.

So-La Says: The two usual ways of playing a string instrument are: bowed or plucked (*pizzicato* - pluck the strings)

, **breath mark** means take a breath, and/or a slight pause or lift.

⊓ **down bow** means on a bowed string instrument, play the note while drawing the bow downward.

V **up bow** means on a bowed string instrument, play the note while drawing the bow upward.

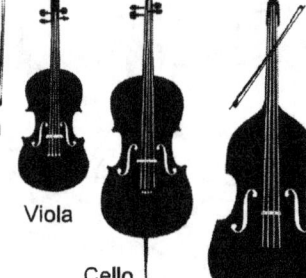

Violin
Viola
Cello
Double Bass

This excerpt (passage or segment) from "The Happy Farmer" by Robert Schumann is notated for violin.

1. Identify and explain the music sign at each of the following letters:

   a) At the letter A: *up bow means on a bowed string instrument, play the note while drawing the bow upward.*

   b) At the letter B: *down bow means on a bowed string instrument, play the note while drawing the bow downward.*

   c) At the letter C: *breath mark means take a breath, and/or a slight pause or lift.*

MUSICAL TERMS WITH A SUFFIX -ETTO and -ISSIMO

The meaning of a **Musical Term** may be changed by adding a suffix (a letter or group of letters) to the end of the word to form a new word. Two common suffixes are -*etto* and -*issimo*.

The suffix -*etto* means to decrease the intensity, "not as". *Allegro* - fast. *Allegretto* - not as fast as allegro.

The suffix -*issimo* means to increase the intensity, "very". *Presto* - fast. *Prestissimo* - very fast.

 So-La Says: Review the Musical Terms, Definitions and Signs in Lesson 12 of the Basic Rudiments Workbook:

Articulation, Signs, Terms, Tempo, Changes in Tempo, Dynamics and Stylistic (Style in Performance).

1. Complete the following for each of the terms below. a) Explain the meaning of the term.
   b) Identify the term as: Articulation, Sign, Term, Tempo, Change in Tempo, Dynamic or Stylistic.

Term	a) Meaning	b) Category
vivace	lively, brisk	Tempo
staccato	sharply detached	Articulation
diminuendo	becoming softer	Dynamic
espressivo	expressive, with expression	Stylistic
pianissimo	very soft	Dynamic
allegretto	not as fast as allegro	Tempo
molto	much, very	Term
prestissimo	as fast as possible	Tempo
rubato	Some freedom of tempo to enhance musical expression	Change in Tempo
mezzo forte	Moderately loud	Dynamic
andantino	a little faster than andante	Tempo
,	take a breath and/or slight pause	Sign
poco	little	Term
tranquillo	quiet, tranquil	Stylistic
larghetto	not as slow as largo	Tempo
leggiero	light, nimble, quick	Articulation
𝄋	dal segno, D.S. from the sign	Sign
spiritoso	spirited	Stylistic

TRANSPOSING - UP OR DOWN ONE OCTAVE INCLUDING CHANGE OF CLEF

Different instruments and voices have a different range of notes or pitches that they can play or sing. **Transposing** music into their range makes it possible for them to play or sing within their register (range).

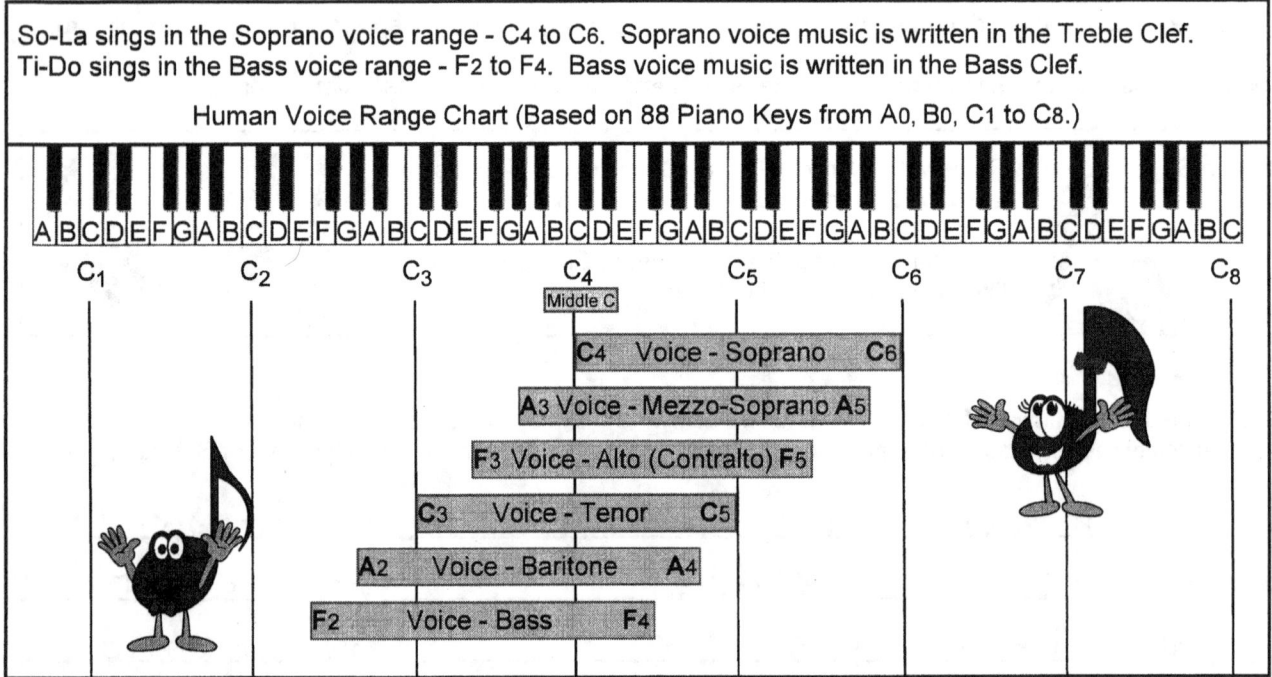

So-La sings in the Soprano voice range - C_4 to C_6. Soprano voice music is written in the Treble Clef.
Ti-Do sings in the Bass voice range - F_2 to F_4. Bass voice music is written in the Bass Clef.

Human Voice Range Chart (Based on 88 Piano Keys from A_0, B_0, C_1 to C_8.)

1. Name the key. Transpose the melody up one octave into the Treble Clef. (So-La Sings Soprano)

Key: F Major

2. Name the key. Transpose the melody down one octave into the Bass Clef. (Ti-Do Sings Bass)

Key: G Major

REWRITING MELODIES AT THE SAME PITCH IN THE ALTERNATE CLEF

Musicians read music in a specific clef based on the range of notes or pitches their instrument produces. **Rewriting** music in an alternate clef makes it easier to read the music on the staff in a specific clef.

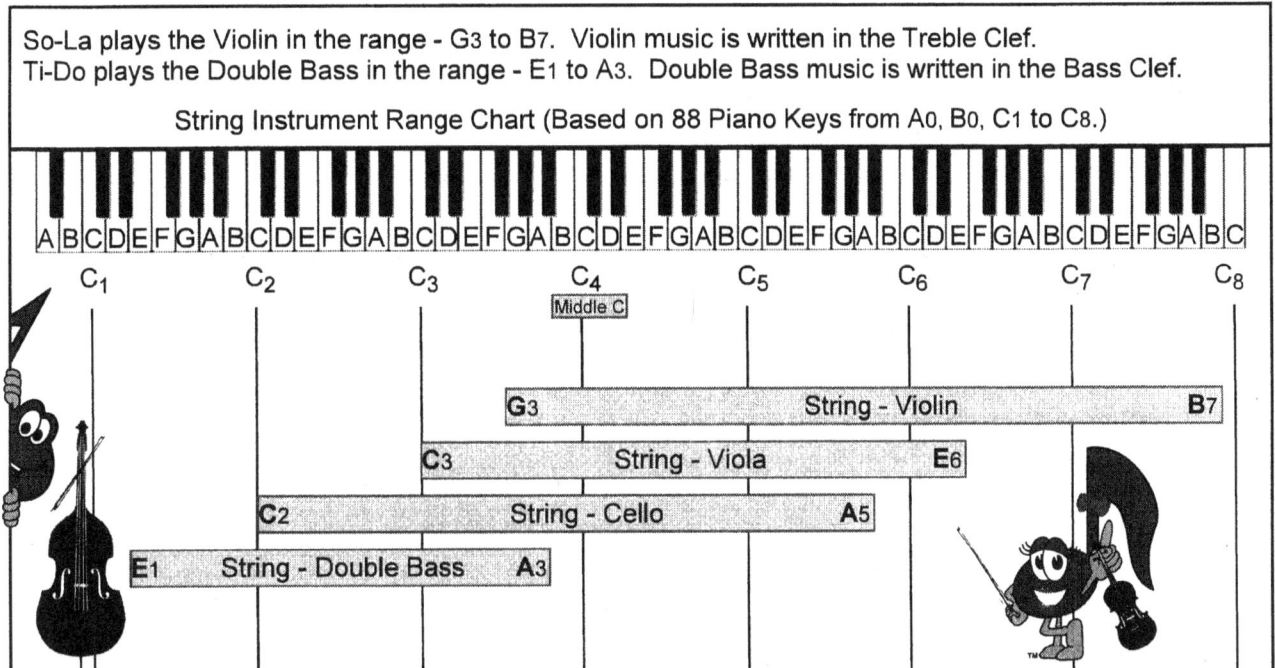

1. Name the key. Rewrite the melody at the same pitch in the Treble Clef. (So-La Plays Violin)

Key: D Major

2. Name the key. Rewrite the melody at the same pitch in the Bass Clef. (Ti-Do Plays Double Bass)

Key: D Major

COMPOSITION of a TWO-MEASURE PHRASE - QUESTION & ANSWER

A melody may consist of a **Two-Measure Question phrase** followed by a **Two-Measure Answer phrase**.

So-La Says: Review the Composition Elements of Melody Writing in the Ultimate Music Theory Level 4 Supplemental Workbook:

Motive, Repetition of Melodic and/or Rhythmic Motive, Phrase and Melody Writing ending on a Stable Scale Degree $\hat{1}$ or $\hat{3}$.

♫ **Ti-Do Tip:** The last note of the Answer phrase, stable scale degree $\hat{1}$, may end on strong beat 1. Move in stepwise motion from the Supertonic $\hat{2}$ to the Tonic $\hat{1}$, or the Leading Tone $\hat{7}$ to the Tonic $\hat{1}$ ($\hat{8}$).

1. Each melody is written in a Major key. Following the examples below, complete each melody with a two-measure Answer phrase. Use the given rhythm. Draw a phrase mark (slur) over the Answer phrase.

   a) In each first melody, end in stepwise motion from the Supertonic $\hat{2}$ down to the Tonic $\hat{1}$.

   b) In each second melody, end in stepwise motion from the Leading Tone $\hat{7}$ up to the Tonic $\hat{1}$ ($\hat{8}$).

(one possible answer for each Question below)

♫ **Ti-Do Time:** Play your compositions. Listen to the Question and different Answer phrases.

COMPOSITION of a FOUR-MEASURE PHRASE - QUESTION & ANSWER - PARALLEL PERIOD

A melody may consist of a **Four-Measure Question phrase** followed by a **Four-Measure Answer phrase**.

A phrase is like a musical sentence. A phrase punctuates the music by ending with a question or comma that indicates more to come, or a period that indicates the end. A Parallel Period (or Sentence) consists of 2 phrases beginning with the same melodic pattern with the second phrase ending on a stable scale degree.

So-La Says: A **Parallel Period** is usually eight measures and contains two four-measure phrases.

The first four-measure phrase is called the **Antecedent**.

Antecedent - Asks the Question. A Question phrase may end on an unstable scale degree ($\hat{2}$ or $\hat{7}$). A question sounds unfinished, open.

The second four-measure phrase is called the **Consequent**.

Consequent - Concludes the Answer. An Answer phrase may end on a stable scale degree ($\hat{1}$ or $\hat{3}$). An answer sounds final, closed.

---

1. Each melody is written in a Major key. Following the example below, complete each melody with a four-measure Answer phrase. Use the given rhythm. Draw a phrase mark over the Answer phrase.

   a) In each Question phrase, label the final note above the staff as unstable scale degree $\hat{2}$ or $\hat{7}$.

   b) In each Answer phrase, create a Parallel Period (phrase beginning with the same melodic pattern). Copy the melodic pattern in mm. 1 - 2 from the Question phrase into mm. 5 - 6 of the Answer phrase.

   c) Complete the Answer phrase ending on the Tonic. Label the stable scale degree $\hat{1}$ above the staff.

   (one possible answer for each Question below)

COMPOSITION of a MELODY ENDING on a STABLE SCALE DEGREE

A Melody usually ends on a **Stable Scale Degree** $\hat{1}$ (Tonic) or $\hat{3}$ (Mediant), which sounds finished (the end). A melody may ascend or descend to approach the final note, $\hat{1}$ or $\hat{3}$, bringing the music to a conclusion.

So-La Says: When writing a melody, sing or play the melody on your instrument to hear if the final note sounds better ending on stable scale degree $\hat{1}$ (Tonic) or stable scale degree $\hat{3}$ (Mediant).

When ending on degree $\hat{1}$, the melody may approach the final note by:

Ascending stepwise motion from degree $\hat{7}$ up to $\hat{8}$ ($\hat{1}$) or
Descending stepwise motion from degree $\hat{2}$ down to $\hat{1}$.

When ending on degree $\hat{3}$, the melody may approach the final note by:

Ascending stepwise motion from degree $\hat{2}$ up to $\hat{3}$ or
Descending stepwise motion from $\hat{4}$ down to $\hat{3}$ or by skip from $\hat{5}$ down to $\hat{3}$.

♫ **Ti-Do Tip:** A melody ending on stable scale degree $\hat{1}$ is a stronger conclusive ending than a melody ending on stable scale degree $\hat{3}$.

1. Each melody is written in a Major key. Following the example below, complete each melody with a four-measure Answer phrase. Use the given rhythm. Draw a phrase mark over the Answer phrase.

   a) In each Question phrase, label the final note above the staff as unstable scale degree $\hat{2}$ or $\hat{7}$.

   b) In each Answer phrase, create a Parallel Period (phrase beginning with the same melodic pattern). Copy the melodic pattern in mm. 1 - 2 from the Question phrase into mm. 5 - 6 of the Answer phrase.

   c) Complete the Answer phrase ending on the Mediant. Label the stable scale degree $\hat{3}$ above the staff.
   (one possible answer for each Question below)

COMPOSITION of a FOUR MEASURE ANSWER PHRASE

A **Composition** (melody writing) may be written using a four-measure Question (antecedent) phrase and a four-measure Answer (consequent) phrase creating a Parallel Period and ending on a stable scale degree.

1. For each of the following melodies, name the key.

    a) Draw a phrase mark (slur) over the given Question phrase. Label the scale degree number directly above the final note of the Question phrase.

    b) Compose a four-measure Answer phrase ending on a stable scale degree. Draw a phrase mark (slur) over the Answer phrase. Label the scale degree number $\hat{1}$ or $\hat{3}$ directly above the final note.

(one possible answer for each Question)

Key: F Major

Key: D Major

Key: g minor

♫ **Ti-Do Tip:** Play your three compositions. Listen to the Question and Answer phrases.

ANALYSIS - MELODY and CHORDS

A melody may outline the Primary Chords (I, i, IV, iv, V or V⁷) of a Major or minor key.

So-La Says: A melody may move by skip or leap, outlining chords in root position or inversions, ascending or descending. (Not all notes of the chord have to be used.) Non-triad notes or Passing Tones (pt) connect triad tones with stepwise motion, moving in the same direction.

The following melody is in the key of C Major. It outlines the C (I), F (IV) and G (V) chords.

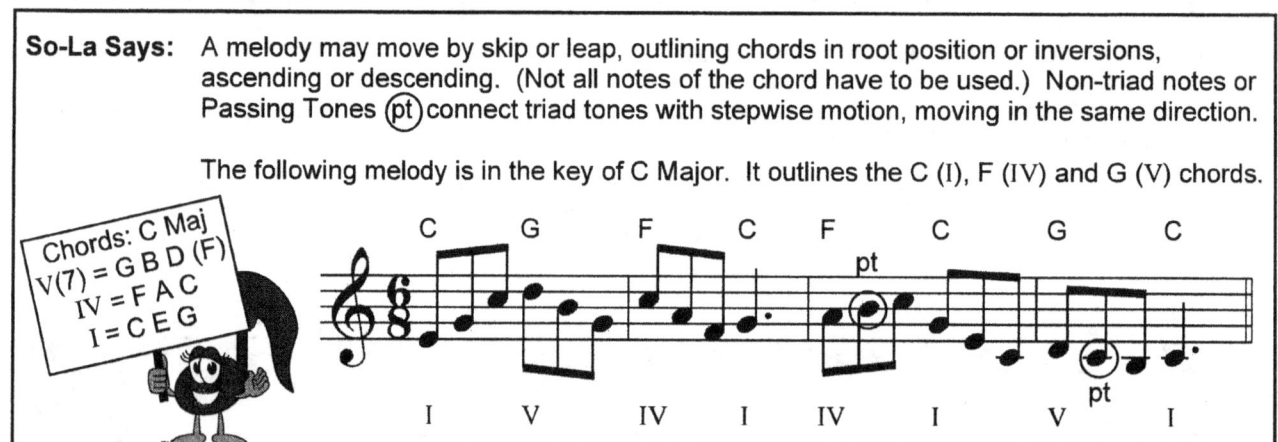

♫ **Ti-Do Tip:** Play the melody above with your *mano destra* (RH) while playing the chords indicated by the Root/Quality Chord Symbols with your *mano sinistra* (LH). Listen to the harmony.

To easily identify the notes for each chord, use the UMT Whiteboard to create a **Chord Chart** for each Key.

When outlining a single staff melody with Chord Symbols, it is **not necessary** to indicate any inversions.

1. Analyze the melodies below. Name the key. Write the Root/Quality Chord Symbol above the staff. Write the Functional Chord Symbol (I, i, IV, iv, V or V⁷) below the staff. Circle and label passing tones as pt.

ANALYSIS - MELODIC PHRASES - UNITY, VARIETY and CONTRAST

A **melodic phrase** may repeat a melodic and/or rhythmic pattern in a same, similar or different manner to create unity, variety and contrast in the music. Achieving balance of these elements creates musical interest.

A melodic phrase is a musical sentence (2 - 4 measures or more) and may include articulation markings: slur, staccato, tenuto, fermata, accent, etc.

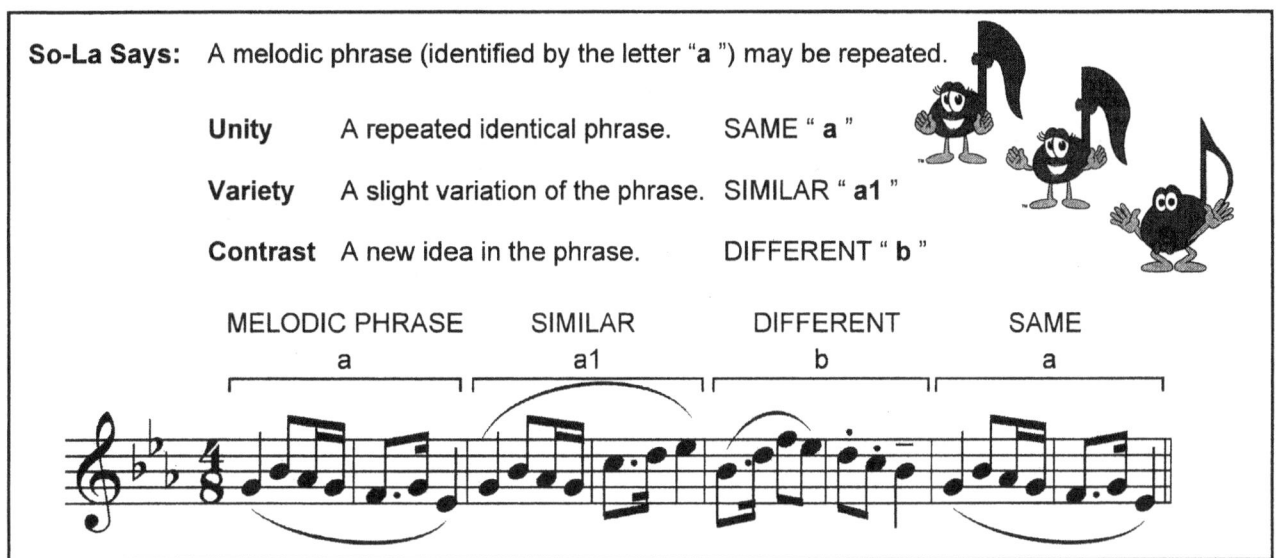

♫ **Ti-Do Tip:** A slur, indicating to play the notes legato, may also be called a phrase (slur) marking.

1. Identify each of the melodic phrases as: a (same), a1 (similar), or b (different).

FORM and ANALYSIS - IDENTIFICATION of CONCEPTS

Form and Analysis of a Melody includes identification of concepts such as Key Signature, Time Signature, Melodic Phrases (a, a1 or b), phrases ending on stable and unstable scale degrees (pitch), tempo, etc.

So-La Says: Always analyze the music before you play it.

Identifying the form and the composer's directions (articulation, signs, terms, tempo, changes in tempo, dynamics and style in performance) help us interpret the music.

♪ **Ti-Do Tip:** Analyze And Play, On Track You Will Stay, Well On Your Way!

1. Analyze the music by answering the questions below. Play the melody.

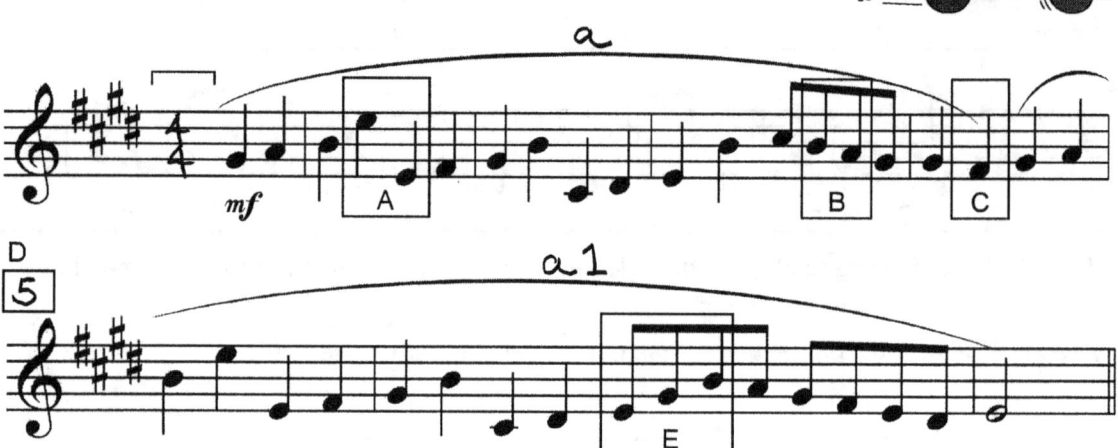

a) Name the key of this piece. __E Major__   Add the correct Time Signature directly on the music.

b) On which beat does this piece begin? __3__   How many beats are in measure 1? __4__

c) Name the interval at the letter A. __Per 8__   Name the interval at the letter B. __Maj 2__

d) Give the technical degree name for the note at the letter C. __Supertonic__   Name the note. __F#__

e) Circle if the first phrase ending is on: a stable scale degree   or   (an unstable scale degree)

f) Write the measure number directly in the square box at the letter D.

g) Directly above each phrase, label each melodic phrase as: a (same), a1 (similar), or b (different).

h) For the triad at the letter E, identify the following: Root: __E__   Type/Quality: __Major__

Position: __root pos__   Root/Quality Chord Symbol: __E__   Functional Chord Symbol: __I__

i) Circle if the second phrase ending is on: (a stable scale degree) or an unstable scale degree.

ANALYSIS - PARALLEL PERIOD

A **Parallel Period** is when a four-measure Question phrase "a" (ending on an unstable scale degree) and a four-measure Answer phrase "a1" (ending on a stable scale degree) have the **same melodic pattern** in the first **2 measures** of both the Question phrase and the Answer phrase.

A four-measure phrase "a" followed by a **different** four-measure phrase "b" is NOT a Parallel Period.

1. Analyze the music by answering the questions below. Play the melody.

a) Name the key of this piece. __C Major__ Add the correct Time Signature directly on the music.

b) Directly above each phrase, label each melodic phrase as: a (same), a1 (similar), or b (different).

c) Identify the measure numbers of the Question phrase: measure __1__ to measure __4__

d) Identify the measure numbers of the Answer phrase: measure __5__ to measure __8__

e) The Question phrase and Answer phrase pairs create a __Parallel__ Period.

f) For the chord at the letter A, identify the following: Root: __G__ Type/Quality: __Dominant 7th__

   Position: __root pos__ Root/Quality Chord Symbol: __G7__ Functional Chord Symbol: __V7__

g) For the chord at the letter B, identify the following: Root: __C__ Type/Quality: __Major__

   Position: __1st inv__ Root/Quality Chord Symbol: __C/E__ Functional Chord Symbol: __I$^6_3$__

IMAGINE, COMPOSE, EXPLORE

♪ **I**magine - Use your imagination to create a title that describes your composition.
♪ **C**ompose - Write your composition and add your name (top right) as the co-composer.
♪ **E**xplore - Add "So-La Sparkles" (terms & signs) to express how the music is played.

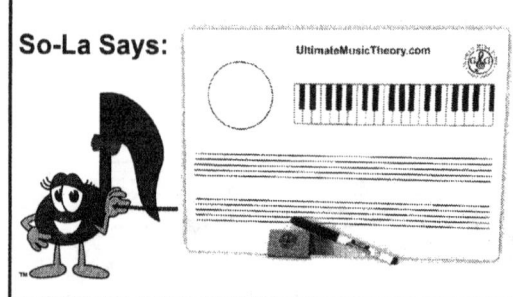

So-La Says:

When composing follow these 3 Composing Steps:

1. Record your melody as you play. Use it as a reference.
2. Write your melody on the Whiteboard. Try different ideas.
3. Write your melody in the workbook. Add "So-La Sparkles" of articulation, dynamics, etc. to create your final composition.

1. Compose a four-measure Answer phrase for the given Question phrase to complete the parallel period.

   a) Name the key. Complete the title of the piece at the top. Add your name as the co-composer.
   b) Draw a phrase mark (slur) over the given phrase. Label the degree number of the final note.
   c) Compose the Answer phrase ending on a stable scale degree. Draw a phrase mark (slur) over the Answer phrase. Label the degree number of the final note of the piece.
   d) Add "So-La Sparkles" using dynamics, articulation, terms, etc. Play your composition.

Blowing Bubbles with Yogi and Boo Boo (title)

Glory St. Germain and Shelagh McKibbon-U'Ren (composers)

Key: B♭ Major

♪ **Ti-Do Time:** Get your "Composers Certificate". SCAN your composition (on this page) and send it to us at: info@ultimatemusictheory.com and we will send you a special **Ultimate Music Theory Composers Certificate** - FREE.

ANALYSIS and SIGHT READING

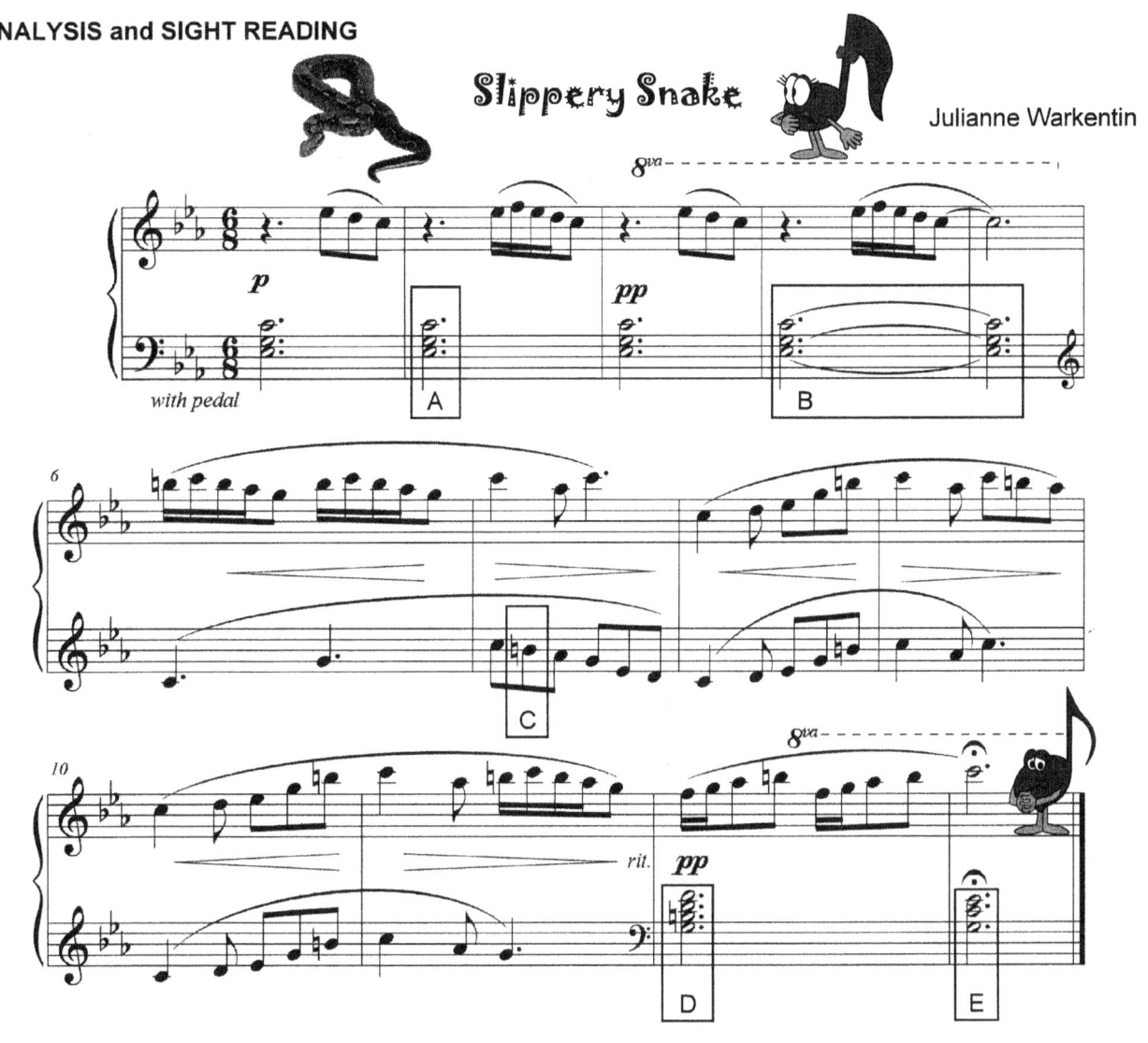

1. Analyze the music by answering the questions below. Play (Sight Read) the piece "Slippery Snake".

    a) Name the key. __C minor__ Identify how many beats are in the first measure. __6__

    b) For the chord at letter A, give the technical degree name of the root note. __Tonic__

    c) Circle the number of beats given to the combined tied notes at letter B: 4   or   6   or ⓬

    d) Name the note at letter C. __B♮__ Explain the natural sign. __raised 7th note of C minor__

    e) Circle if the phrases at mm. 8 - 9 and mm. 10 - 11 are: same (a)   or   (similar (a1))   or   different (b).

    f) For the chord at the letter D, identify the following: Root: __G__   Type/Quality: __Dominant 7th__

       Position: __root pos__   Root/Quality Chord Symbol: __G⁷__   Functional Chord Symbol: __V⁷__

    g) For the chord at the letter E, identify the following: Root: __C__   Type/Quality: __minor__

       Position: __2nd inv__   Root/Quality Chord Symbol: __Cm/G__   Functional Chord Symbol: __i⁶₄__

MUSIC HISTORY - VOICES IN VOCAL MUSIC

Orchestral Instruments are divided into sections (families): String, Woodwind, Brass, Percussion and Other. **Modern Vocal Music** (or SATB Music) is divided into specific vocal ranges: Soprano, Alto, Tenor and Bass.

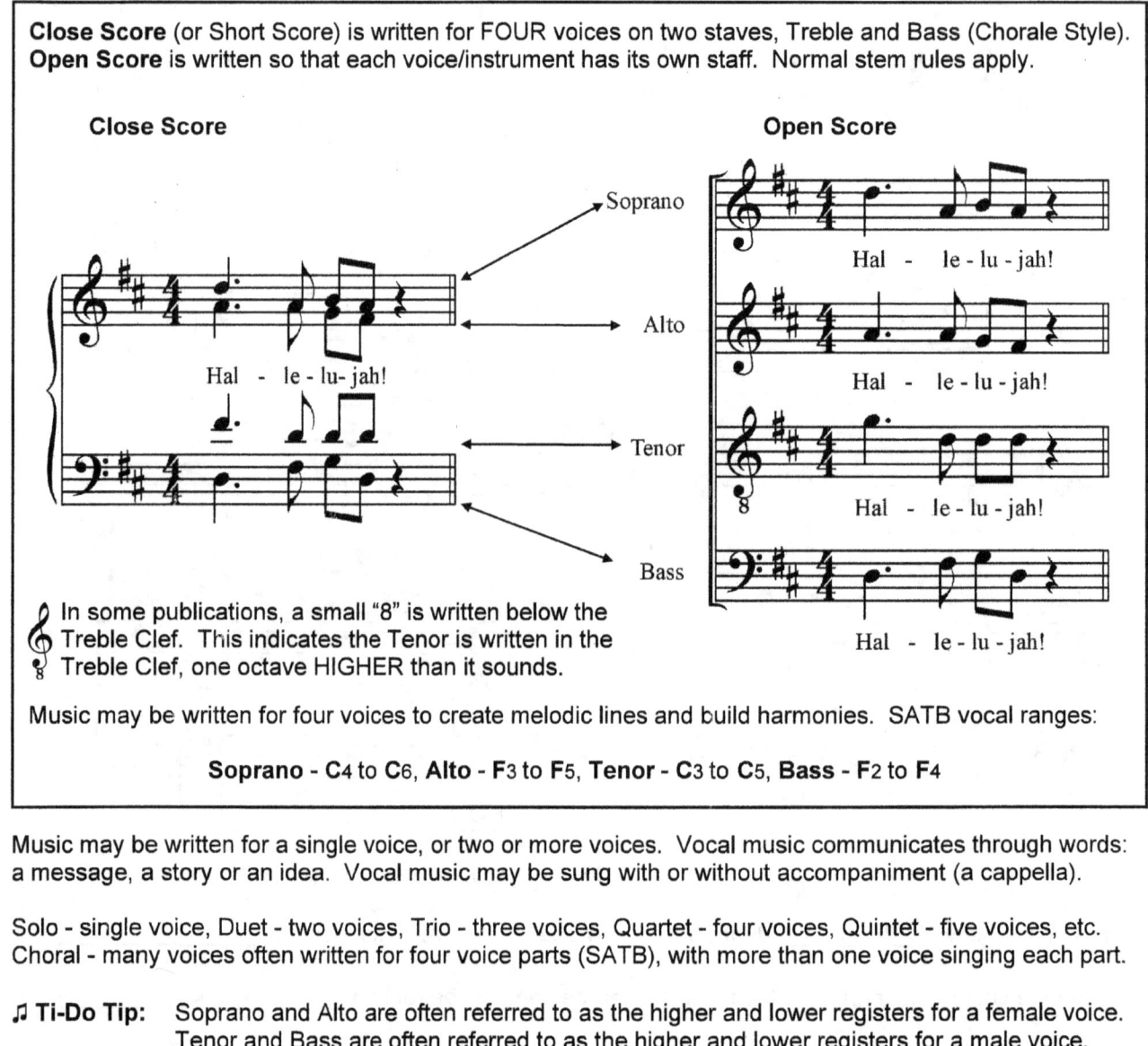

Close Score (or Short Score) is written for FOUR voices on two staves, Treble and Bass (Chorale Style).
Open Score is written so that each voice/instrument has its own staff. Normal stem rules apply.

In some publications, a small "8" is written below the Treble Clef. This indicates the Tenor is written in the Treble Clef, one octave HIGHER than it sounds.

Music may be written for four voices to create melodic lines and build harmonies. SATB vocal ranges:

Soprano - C4 to C6, **Alto** - F3 to F5, **Tenor** - C3 to C5, **Bass** - F2 to F4

Music may be written for a single voice, or two or more voices. Vocal music communicates through words: a message, a story or an idea. Vocal music may be sung with or without accompaniment (a cappella).

Solo - single voice, Duet - two voices, Trio - three voices, Quartet - four voices, Quintet - five voices, etc.
Choral - many voices often written for four voice parts (SATB), with more than one voice singing each part.

♫ **Ti-Do Tip:** Soprano and Alto are often referred to as the higher and lower registers for a female voice. Tenor and Bass are often referred to as the higher and lower registers for a male voice.

Male or Female voices may sing **any vocal part** provided it is within their **own vocal range**.

Go to **GSGMUSIC.com** - For Easy Access to listening to male and female voices singing in various ranges.

1. Name the four voices identified as SATB: _Soprano_, _Alto_, _Tenor_, _Bass_

2. Music written for four voices on two staves is called ___Close___ Score.

3. Music written for four voices, with each voice on it's own staff, is called ___Open___ Score.

4. True or False - Female voices ONLY sing in the vocal range of Soprano or Alto. ___False___

5. True or False - Male voices ONLY sing in the vocal range of Tenor or Bass. ___False___

MUSIC HISTORY - GENRE, PERFORMING FORCES and RELATIONSHIP BETWEEN MUSIC & TEXT

Genre is a classification system used to describe and define the standard category and overall character of a work. A Genre is characterized by similarities in form, style, type, musical period, subject matter, etc.

Opera - A Genre of Music defined as a dramatic production of a story, performed in a concert setting. Performers include solo singers, a chorus and an orchestra. There are costumes, scenery, lights, dancing (ballet), singing, acting and action. Opera has been a big part of music history in Europe since the 1600s.

Oratorio - A Genre of Music defined as a production of a Biblical or religious story, performed in a church or concert hall. Performers include solo singers, a chorus and an orchestra. There are NO costumes, scenery or dramatic action. Oratorios reached their peak of popularity in the 1700s, and are still performed today.

An Oratorio and an Opera both include the following elements:

- **Overture** - An introductory movement for orchestra, often presenting melodies from arias to come.
- **Recitative** - A melodic speech sung by a narrator to tell the story and to quickly advance the plot.
- **Aria** - A lyric song for solo voice with orchestral accompaniment, expressing intense emotion in the story.
- **Chorus** - A large group of singers performing together in various voice parts (SATB).
- **Libretto** - The Italian term meaning a "little book" is the text of the story of an oratorio or an opera.

Vocal Music - The oldest Genre of Music, this Genre is defined as music performed by one or more singers, with or without accompaniment, in which the singing (voice) is the main focus of the piece. There are many forms (styles, types) of music within this Genre, including Barbershop, Standards, Vocal Jazz, etc.

Verse - Chorus Structure - A form (type) of Vocal Music that became popular in the 20th/21st Century. In this form of Vocal Music, each Verse (stanza) develops the story line and the Chorus (refrain) is repeated at the end of each Verse. The text of each Verse is different and the text of each Chorus is the same.

Performing Forces - The term "Performing Forces" indicates the instruments or voice types used to perform a work, a piece or a song.

When the Performing Forces are a solo singer, violin and piano, each of the Performing Forces can be identified by their unique Tone Color.

Relationship between Music & Text - For music to connect to the text, when the text (words) being sung indicate sorrow, despair, love, excitement, triumph, etc., the music must support the message.

Music can enhance the relationship to the text through tonality, melody, harmony, texture, rhythm, dynamics, tempo, articulation, etc.

Go to **GSGMUSIC.com** - For Easy Access to Videos in all Genres. Listen & Identify the Performing Forces.

1. Name the term for the classification system used to describe the overall character of a work. **Genre**
2. Name the Genre that includes orchestra and singers, but does not use costumes. **Oratorio**
3. Name the Genre that includes orchestra, singers, costume and acting. **Opera**
4. Name the Genre where the musical focus is on the singing. **Vocal Music**
5. Name the type of Vocal Music that uses stanzas and refrains. **Verse - Chorus Structure**

MUSIC HISTORY - GEORGE FRIDERIC HANDEL

George Frideric Handel (1685 - 1759) was one of two composing giants of the Baroque Era (1600 - 1750). The other was J.S. Bach. Handel, born in Germany, traveled to Italy and England to pursue his career. He played violin, harpsichord, organ & oboe, and earned fame composing Italian operas and English oratorios.

Handel composed more that 26 Oratorios, the most famous choral work "Messiah" was composed in only 24 days in (August & September of) 1741.

The Genre of Messiah is an Oratorio consisting of 53 sections: 19 choruses, 16 arias, 16 recitatives and 2 sections for orchestra alone.

Most Oratorios are based on biblical stories. The Libretto for the Messiah was compiled by Charles Jennens using text from the Bible.

Hallelujah Chorus from Messiah was first performed in London for King George II, who was so impressed when he heard the "Hallelujah Chorus" that he stood up! When the King stood up, everyone stood up - a tradition that continues to this day.

The word chorus has two meanings. 1. A chorus is a choral section of a large work such as an oratorio or an opera. 2. A chorus is a large group of people that sing choral music. In fact, a chorus may sing a chorus!

The Hallelujah Chorus (choral section of a large work) is sung by the chorus (large group of people).

Messiah tells the story of Jesus Christ in 3 Parts (based upon the liturgical calendar of the Church). Each of the 3 Parts contains many sections and movements:

Part One – Christmas (the prophecy of the coming of Christ and his birth)
Part Two – Easter (Christ's suffering, death and the spread of his doctrine)
Part Three – Redemption (the redemption of the world through faith)

The **Hallelujah Chorus** is featured in the final Scene (#7) of Part Two of Messiah.

The majestic opening features all SATB Chorus Voices singing the same word ("Hallelujah) using the same rhythm. This creates a forceful chordal (solid, blocked) Harmonic Texture.

The repetition of key words such as "Hallelujah" and "forever" create a dramatic, emotional context.

Go to **GSGMUSIC.com** - For Easy Access to videos for listening to the Hallelujah Chorus from Messiah.

1. Listen to Handel's Messiah: Hallelujah Chorus. Check (✓) the correct answer to the questions below.

Performing Forces in the Hallelujah Chorus are:	
☐ Orchestral Instruments Only	☑ SATB Chorus & Orchestra

The composer of Messiah - Hallelujah Chorus is:	
☑ G.F. Handel	☐ J.S. Bach

The Genre of Messiah is an:	
☐ Opera	☑ Oratorio

MUSIC HISTORY - HALLELUJAH CHORUS FROM MESSIAH

The relationship between text (words) and music is truly the language of music. Music is used to communicate a message, emotion or tell a story. How text is articulated and expressed within the rhythmic, melodic and harmonic patterns of the music affects our emotional connection and experience.

 In the Baroque Era, when Handel wrote the Hallelujah Chorus from Messiah, there were no computers, music writing programs or photocopiers.

Composers had to hand write the music for each instrument and voice part. The original composition was then carefully rewritten by hand by music copyists, who were employed to produce neat copies from a composer's manuscript.

One relationship in music is the relationship between the text (words) and the music (instruments). This is a musical technique called **Word Painting**, Text Painting or Tone Painting. This device specifically refers to when the music reflects the literal meaning of the text.

Word Painting may be expressed through the rhythmic patterns, melodic direction (pitch) or note values. In Handel's Hallelujah Chorus, the relationship between text and music is evident as the music tries to imitate the emotion, action and sounds as described in the text.

1. For each of the excepts below, identify the Word Painting, the relationship between the text and the music, as through: melodic direction (pitch), rhythmic pattern, or note values.

Text: The Kingdom of this world.

Relationship: "Kingdom" is sung at a higher pitch (representing Heaven) and the melodic direction descends down to the "world", which is sung at a lower pitch (representing the Earth).

The King - dom of   this   world

a) The relationship between the text and the music is through: _melodic direction (pitch)_

Text: And He shall reign forever and ever.

Relationship: The rhythmic pattern starts as **syllabic** (one syllable of text per note). Then the rhythm changes to **melismatic** (one syllable over several different notes) emphasizing the importance of "Forever".

And He shall reign for-ev-er and ev - - - er.

b) The relationship between the text and the music is through: _rhythmic pattern_

Text: King of Kings, and Lord of Lords.

Relationship: The note values given to "Kings" and "Lords" is held longer and stresses the importance of God being THE King and THE Lord.

King of Kings,   and Lord of Lords.

c) The relationship between the text and the music is through: _note values_

MUSIC HISTORY - WOLFGANG AMADEUS MOZART

Wolfgang Amadeus Mozart (1756 - 1791) was a genius composer from the Classical Era (1750 - 1825). Opera was his favorite Genre of music. He also wrote great works for piano, voice, orchestra and chamber music. In the Level 2 Supplemental, you learned about the talented and gifted young Mozart and his music.

Mozart's music is a reflection of the man himself, from a mood of humor to noble tragedy, from simplicity to elegant brilliance and complex forms.

Mozart was commissioned to add wind parts to Handel's Messiah and other operatic works. This led Mozart to study the contrapuntal works of Handel and J.S. Bach, inspiring him to write his most adventurous styles of harmonic music.

Mozart's The Magic Flute *(Die Zauberflöte)* was his last opera. The Queen of the Night Aria is from Act 2 of The Magic Flute (libretto by Emanuel Schikaneder).

The Magic Flute is a testament to the many sides of Mozart and includes comedy, brilliant arias, folklike melodies, emotional drama and noble choral ensembles.

Mozart wrote for specific voice ranges. The music symbolically represents each distinctive character and covered all vocal ranges of SATB (and others): Prince Tamino (tenor), Papageno the birdcatcher (baritone), Pamina the Queens daughter (soprano), Sarastro the high priest (bass), Monostatos the servant (tenor), 3 Ladies (sopranos, mezzo-soprano), 3 Spirits - written for boys (treble, alto and mezzo-soprano), etc.

Mozart's Opera "The Magic Flute" (K. 620) is a fairy tale with themes of love and of good versus evil. The opera is divided into 2 Acts. Act 1 has 4 scenes, Act 2 has 10 Scenes. In Act 2, Scene 3, there are 3 Arias:

Aria #1: "Alles fühlt der Liebe Freuden" ("Everyone feels the joys of love") - Monostatos, Sarastro's servant, gazes upon the sleeping Pamina and laments that she cannot love him like he loves her, because he is only a lowly servant. He goes to kiss her, but the Queen enters!

Aria #2: "Der Hölle Rache kocht in meinem Herzen" ("My heart is seething with hellish vengeance") - The Queen (Pamina's mother) is angry that Sarastro kidnapped her daughter. She gives Pamina a dagger and orders her to kill him. Her need for revenge is so great, she threatens to disown Pamina if she doesn't do it. (This Aria became so popular, it was known simply as the "Queen of the Night" Aria.)

Aria #3: "In diesen heil'gen Hallen" ("Within these sacred portals revenge is unknown") - Pamina begs Sarastro to forgive her mother. He reassures her that revenge and cruelty have no place in his heart.

Go to **GSGMUSIC.com** - For Easy Access to videos for listening to Mozart's Queen of the Night.

1. Listen to Mozart's Queen of the Night Aria from The Magic Flute: Check (✓) the correct answer below.

Performing Forces in the Queen of the Night Aria are:	
✓ Coloratura Soprano & Orchestra	☐ SATB Chorus & Orchestra

The melody of the Queen of the Night is:	
✓ aggressive, staccato, melismatic	☐ dolce, legato, syllabic

The Genre of The Magic Flute is an:	
✓ Opera	☐ Oratorio

MUSIC HISTORY - QUEEN OF THE NIGHT - THE MAGIC FLUTE

Word Painting, the relationship between text (words) and music, builds a powerful emotional connection that transcends the listener into the magical world of their imagination through voices in song and music.

The "Queen of the Night" must be performed by a **Coloratura Soprano**.

This is a Soprano voice that is highly agile, trained to specialize in elaborate vocal ornamentation (large vocal leaps, trills, arpeggios, rapid successions of notes, etc.). A Coloratura Soprano's dramatic and powerful range is anywhere between a C4 to an F6 (and even higher).

Word Painting may be expressed through the relationship of **sound and silence** between the solo voice and the accompaniment to build drama or create suspense. The relationship may be punctuated by matching the **dynamics and articulation** to emphasize a statement, message or emotion.

1. For each of the excepts below, identify the Word Painting, the relationship between the text and the music, as through: sound and silence or dynamics and articulation.

Text: Hear a mother's oath!

Relationship: The Queen of the Night solo voice and all the orchestral instruments come in together on "Hear", but then all the instruments stop and are completely silent.

The Queen's solo voice continues to hold the word "Hear", and then sings "a mother's oath" without any accompaniment (a cappella).

The sound and silence brings force to the strength of this oath - no accompaniment is needed.

a) The relationship between the text and the music is: _sound and silence_

Text: Go forth, and bear (my vengeance)!

Relationship: The dynamic sign is "fp" - a fortepiano - loud on "Go" ("Fühlt") and then soft for the rest of the statement, "forth, and bear…".

The articulation of staccato violin intensifies the direct importance of each word - punctuating each syllable with the depth of her anger.

The matching dynamics and articulation bring unity to the message, which is presented by both voice and accompaniment.

b) The relationship between the text and the music is: _dynamics and articulation_

MUSIC HISTORY - HAROLD ARLEN (born Hyman Arluck)

Harold Arlen (1905 - 1986) was an American composer from the 20th Century Period (1900 - 2000). Arlen studied piano and voice and his dream was to be a performer. By the age of 15, Arlen was performing with his "Snappy Trio" band and spent most of his time performing, arranging, playing the piano and singing.

Arlen is credited with writing over 400 songs including: "One For my Baby", "Get Happy", "Stormy Weather", "That Old Black Magic" and his most beloved "Over the Rainbow", a song in the Vocal Music Genre with a verse - chorus structure.

His music is characterized as rhythm numbers, jazz pieces, ballads and torch songs. He wrote some of the greatest hits from the 30's and 40's including the 1939 movie score for the Wizard of Oz.

Photo Credit: Harold Arlen transferring a "jot" from the small pad on the left to a piano copy while dog, Shmutts, observes. Used with Permission from SA Music, LLC photo

In 1938, Harold Arlen and Edgar Yipsel Harburg were signed by Metro Goldwyn Mayer (MGM) to write a film score (music) for a movie. Little did Arlen know, it would be the pinnacle of his career - The Wizard of Oz!

In writing the film score (picture songs) Arlen said: "I felt we needed something with a sweep, a melody with a broad, long, line. My feeling was that picture songs need to be lush, and picture songs are hard to write."

Arlen wrote "Over the Rainbow" (lyrics by Harburg), which was deleted from the print of The Wizard of Oz three times! The publisher objected to the "difficult-to-sing" octave leap in the melody on the word "somewhere," and to the simple middle section. Judy Garland (lead role of Dorothy), heard the song and loved it.

The song remained and Over the Rainbow later received the Academy Award as the best film song of the year! In 2000, Over the Rainbow was recognized as the Best Song of the 20th Century.

Go to **GSGMUSIC.com** - For Easy Access to videos for listening to Arlen's Over the Rainbow.

1. Listen to Arlen's Over the Rainbow from The Wizard of Oz: Check (✓) the correct answer below.

The Performing Forces of "Over the Rainbow" from the movie "The Wizard of Oz" are:	
✓ Solo Soprano & Orchestra	☐ SATB Chorus & Orchestra

Harold Arlen was a composer from the:	
☐ Classical Period	✓ 20th Century Period

The Genre of Over the Rainbow is:	
✓ Vocal with Verse - Chorus Structure	☐ An aria from an Oratorio

The composer of the music for Over the Rainbow is:	
☐ Edgar Yipsel Harburg	✓ Harold Arlen

MUSIC HISTORY - OVER THE RAINBOW - THE WIZARD OF OZ

Over the Rainbow is protect by copyright. The first copyright law, known as The Statute of Anne 1710, was an act to protect the creative works of authors, composers, etc., ensuring that they were paid for their work.

Public Domain works are works that have been published 95 years before January 1 of the current year. 20th Century composers such as Arlen have their music protected under copyright laws.

Copyright

The © Copyright symbol indicates an original work. Composers may still hand write their music to notate their ideas and then use various programs to write, record and produce their final musical manuscript.

Various types of music notation and reproducing methods make it easy to photocopy music, which is prohibited unless permission is granted by the copyright holder.

1. For each of the excepts below, identify the Word Painting, the relationship between the text and the music, as through: intervals and direction or rhythmic pattern.

Text: Somewhere over the rainbow, way up high.

Relationship: The octave leap up focuses the voice and the action "up high" (painting the difference between the ground and the sky - where a Rainbow is seen).

Even "way UP high" emphasizes the word "UP" by leaping an interval of a sixth upwards.

Somewhere o - ver the rain-bow, way up high

a) The relationship between the text and the music is: _intervals and direction_

Text: If happy little bluebirds fly beyond the rainbow...

Relationship: The "trilling" of birds is traditionally represented in music by the repeated trilling of notes (oscillating rhythmic pattern - moving quickly back and forth between 2 notes).

The movement up a 2nd in "beyond the rainbow" represents the birds flying higher.

If hap-py lit-tle blue-birds fly be-yond the rainbow

b) The relationship between the text and the music is: _rhythmic pattern_

Write your own text and music. Indicate the relationship. Draw the © Copyright sign, your name and the date at the bottom of your work.

Text: _Stepping Up So High, let's Sing So-La Ti-Do_

Relationship: _Music is moving up by step, interval of a second + singing so-la, ti-do_

Step-ping up so high, let's sing So-La Ti-Do

© Glory St. Germain July 2017

c) The relationship between the text and the music is: _intervals and direction_

MUSIC HISTORY - REVIEW CHART

Throughout music history, composers have explored composition through various genres, using different performing forces or voice types and connecting the relationship between the text and the music.

> Review the synopsis for each of the following compositions. Fill in the blanks using the following terms:
>
> | | | | |
> |---|---|---|---|
> | Over the Rainbow | Oratorio | Coloratura Soprano & Orchestra | G.F. Handel |
> | W.A. Mozart | Hallelujah Chorus | SATB Chorus & Orchestra | H. Arlen |
> | Queen of the Night | Vocal Music | Solo Soprano & Orchestra | Opera |

1. a) Synopsis: The Chorus sings of the jubilation (feelings of great triumph and happiness) that they are experiencing at the resurrection of Jesus Christ, as derived from 3 passages in the book of Revelation.

Composition: __Hallelujah Chorus__   Composer: __G.F. Handel__

Performing Forces or Voice Types: __SATB Chorus + Orchestra__ Genre: __Oratorio__

b) Write one example of the relationship between the text and the music (Word Painting) for this piece.

__text: "Kingdom of this World" music: melodic direction (pitch)__
(one possible answer)

2. a) Synopsis: The explosive dramatic performance of the woman who seeks revenge upon the high priest and calls upon her daughter to kill him. As in traditional fairy tales, goodness prevails at the end.

Composition: __Queen of the Night__   Composer: __W.A. Mozart__

Performing Forces or Voice Types: __Coloratura Soprano + Orchestra__ Genre: __Opera__

b) Write one example of the relationship between the text and the music (Word Painting) for this piece.

__text: "Hear a mother's oath!" music: sound and silence (dramatic)__
(one possible answer)

3. a) Synopsis: A young girl is told to find a place in the barnyard where she won't get into trouble. She dreams about a far away place behind the moon and beyond the rain where life would be adventurous.

Composition: __Over the Rainbow__   Composer: __H. Arlen__

Performing Forces or Voice Types: __Solo Soprano + Orchestra__ Genre: __Vocal Music__

b) Write one example of the relationship between the text and the music (Word Painting) for this piece.

__text: "Way Up High" music: leaping up an interval of a sixth__
(one possible answer)

4. Identify which Composition is sung by the following:

a) __Queen of the Night__ - A coloratura soprano who sings in dramatic, vengeful, melismatic and aggressive rhythms to express her desire for rage.

b) __Over the Rainbow__ - A innocent young soprano who sings in a lyrical, tranquil voice to express her longing and wistful dreams for her life to be different.

c) __Hallelujah Chorus__ - An expansive and triumphant chorus singing in a polyphonic texture of 4-part harmony to express their joy at the majestic resurrection of Jesus Christ.

Ultimate Music Theory
Level 5 Theory Exam

Total Score: ___ / 100

The Ultimate Music Theory™ Rudiments Workbooks, Supplemental Workbooks and Exams prepare students for successful completion of the Royal Conservatory of Music Theory Levels.

1. a) The following melody is from Julianne Warkentin's "Honey Bunny" (Ultimate Peculiar Pets Book). Name the note under each bracket.

/10

b) Write the Enharmonic Equivalent for each note. Use whole notes.

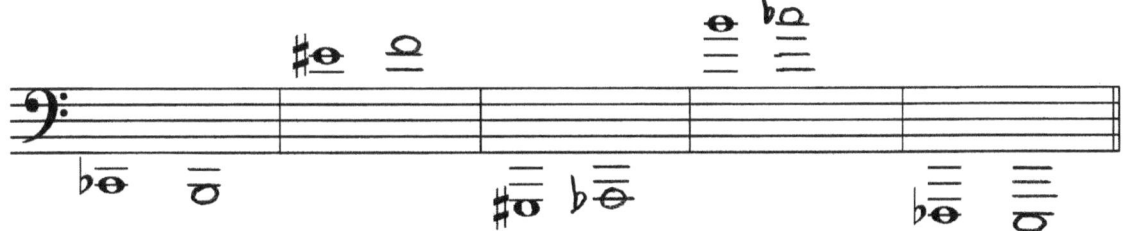

2. Following the first example, for each of the following Time Signatures:
   a) Top Number: Write the number of beats (2, 3, 4 or 6) per measure.
   b) Bottom Number: Draw the kind of note that equals one Basic Beat (half, quarter or eighth note).

/10

2/2 = _2_ beats per measure
2/2 = _𝅗𝅥_ note equals one beat

4/4 = _4_ beats per measure
4/4 = _♩_ note equals one beat

3/2 = _3_ beats per measure
3/2 = _𝅗𝅥_ note equals one beat

2/8 = _2_ beats per measure
2/8 = _♪_ note equals one beat

4/2 = _4_ beats per measure
4/2 = _𝅗𝅥_ note equals one beat

3/8 = _3_ beats per measure
3/8 = _♪_ note equals one beat

2/4 = _2_ beats per measure
2/4 = _♩_ note equals one beat

4/8 = _4_ beats per measure
4/8 = _♪_ note equals one beat

3/4 = _3_ beats per measure
3/4 = _♩_ note equals one beat

6/8 = _6_ beats per measure
6/8 = _♪_ note equals one beat

UltimateMusicTheory.com © Copyright 2017 Gloryland Publishing. All Rights Reserved. 73

Ultimate Music Theory
Level 5 Theory Exam

3. a) Add the rest(s) below each bracket to complete each measure.

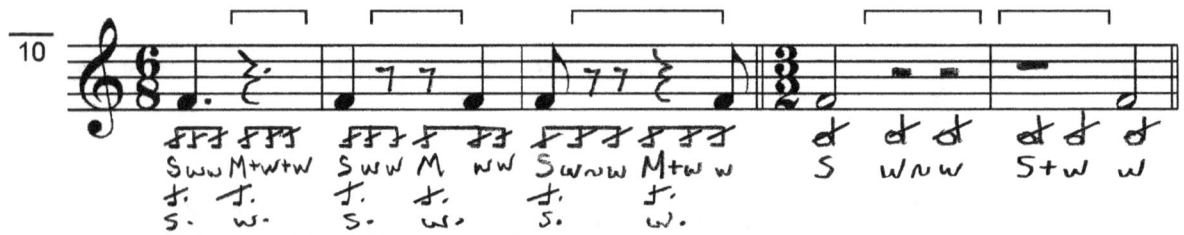

b) Add the correct Time Signature below each bracket.

c) Add the missing bar lines.

4. a) Write the following melodic intervals above each given note. Use whole notes. Use accidentals when necessary. Name both notes of the melodic interval.

b) Name both notes (lower note first) of each harmonic interval. Name the harmonic intervals.

Ultimate Music Theory
Level 5 Theory Exam

5. Name the Major or minor key of each of the following Dominant Seventh Chords.

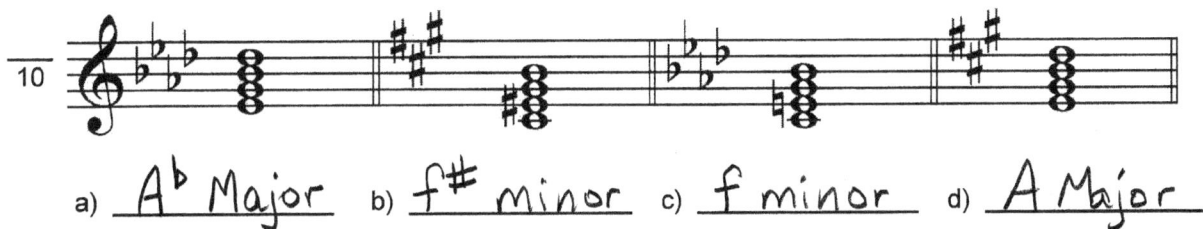

a) A♭ Major   b) f♯ minor   c) f minor   d) A Major

Write the following Solid (Blocked) triads. Use whole notes. Use a Key Signature and any necessary accidentals. Write the Root/Quality Chord Symbol above and the Functional Chord Symbol below.

e) Dominant triad of D Major in second inversion.

Root/Quality Chord Symbol: A/E

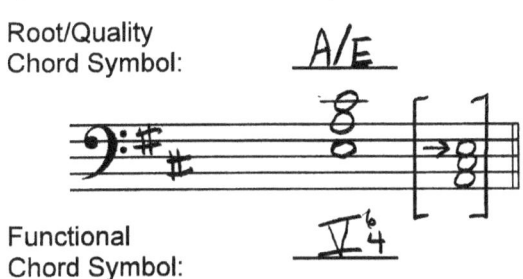

Functional Chord Symbol: V⁶₄

f) Tonic triad of f♯ minor in first inversion.

Root/Quality Chord Symbol: F♯m/A

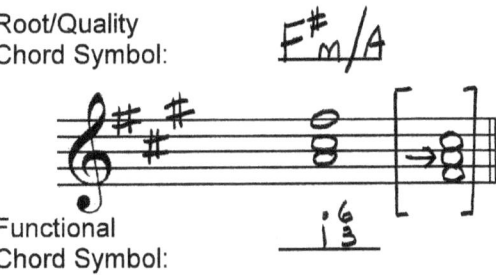

Functional Chord Symbol: i⁶₃

g) Dominant triad of d minor in root position.

Root/Quality Chord Symbol: A

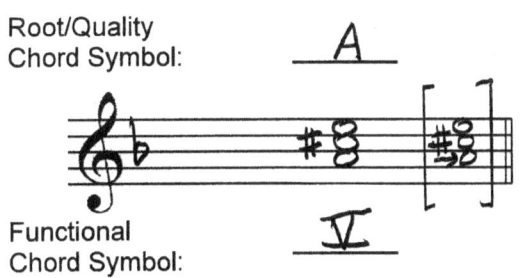

Functional Chord Symbol: V

h) Subdominant triad of c minor in first inversion.

Root/Quality Chord Symbol: Fm/A♭

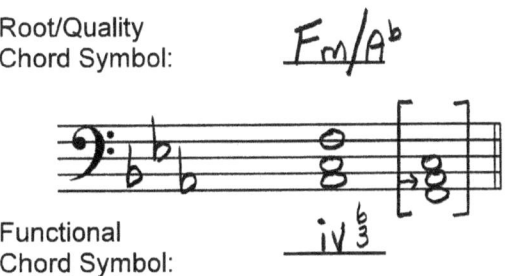

Functional Chord Symbol: iv⁶₃

i) Tonic triad of E♭ Major in second inversion.

Root/Quality Chord Symbol: E♭/B♭

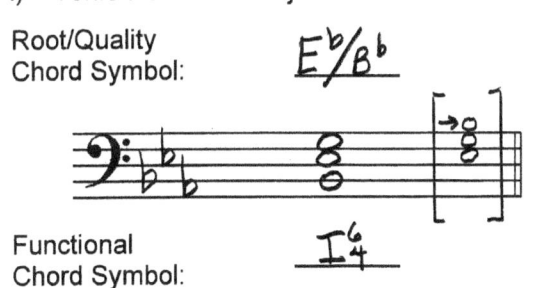

Functional Chord Symbol: I⁶₄

j) Subdominant triad of G Major in root position.

Root/Quality Chord Symbol: C

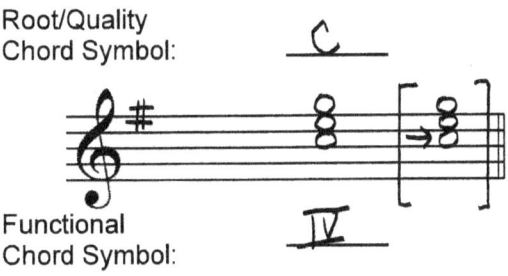

Functional Chord Symbol: IV

Ultimate Music Theory
Level 5 Theory Exam

6. Write the following scales, ascending and descending. Use a Key Signature and any necessary accidentals. Use whole notes.

10 a) The relative minor scale, melodic form, of E Major in the Treble Clef. (c# min mel)

b) The Tonic Major scale (Parallel Major) of c minor in the Bass Clef. (C Major)

c) c minor harmonic scale in the Bass Clef.

d) The relative Major scale of f minor in the Treble Clef. (A♭ Major)

e) The Tonic minor scale (Parallel minor) harmonic form of D Major in the Treble Clef. (d min harm.)

f) Fill in the blanks to identify each of the following note names.

The Leading Tone of b minor harmonic scale: __A#__.

The Subtonic of b minor natural scale: __A__.

The Leading Tone of A flat Major scale: __G__.

The Subdominant of c sharp minor melodic scale: __F#__.

The Dominant of B flat Major scale: __F__.

Ultimate Music Theory
Level 5 Theory Exam

7. a) Name the key of this melody.
    b) Draw a phrase mark (slur) over the given Question phrase. Label the scale degree number of the final note in the Question phrase.
    c) Compose a four-measure Answer phrase to create a Parallel Period. End on a stable scale degree.
    d) Draw a phrase mark over the Answer phrase. Label the scale degree number of the final note.

10

Key: D Major

(one possible answer)

e) Name the key of the following melody.
f) Transpose the melody down one octave into the Bass Clef using the correct Key Signature.

Key: G Major

Ultimate Music Theory
Level 5 Theory Exam

8. Complete the following questions by filling in the blanks.

   __/10

   a) The composer of the "Messiah" is **G.F. Handel**.

   b) The composer of "Over the Rainbow" is **H. Arlen**.

   c) The composer of "The Magic Flute" is **W. A. Mozart**.

   d) One aria from "The Magic Flute" is entitled **Queen of the Night**.

   e) The genre of the "Messiah" is an **Oratorio**.

   f) The "Hallelujah Chorus" is written for **Soprano**, Alto, **Tenor** and Bass.

   g) Writing music that reflects the literal meaning of the words is called **word painting**.

   h) The structure of "Over the Rainbow" is **Verse** - **Chorus**.

   i) A Soprano Voice with extreme agility and range is called a **Coloratura** Soprano.

   j) As featured in the MGM Production of "The Wizard of Oz", the performing forces for "Over the Rainbow" are **solo soprano** and **orchestra**.

9. Match each musical term or sign with the English definition. (Not all definitions will be used.)

   __/10

Term		Definition
tranquillo	c	a) very slow
spiritoso	i	b) lively, brisk
andantino	f	c) quiet, tranquil
rubato	l	d) little
largo	a	e) much, very
leggiero	j	f) a little faster than andante
vivace	b	g) from the beginning
espressivo	k	h) from the sign
dal segno, D.S.	h	i) spirited
molto	e	j) light, nimble, quick
poco	d	k) with expression, expressive
		l) with some freedom of tempo to enhance musical expression

Ultimate Music Theory
Level 5 Theory Exam

10. Analyze the ending of the "Hallelujah Chorus" from the Messiah by answering the questions below.

a) Add the correct Time Signature directly below the bracket. Name the Key. __D Major__

b) Circle the Composer of this excerpt: (Handel)   or   Mozart   or   Arlen

c) Circle if the intervals at the letter A are: Parallel 4ths   or   Parallel 6ths   or   (Parallel 8ths)

d) Identify the interval at the letter B. __Maj 2__   Circle if this interval is: (melodic) or harmonic.

e) Identify the interval at the letter C. __Per 8__   Circle if this interval is: melodic   or (harmonic)

f) Circle if the texture at the letter D is: monophonic   or   homophonic   or (polyphonic)

g) Circle if the triad at letter E is the: Tonic or (Subdominant) or Dominant. Name the root. __G__

h) At the letter F, identify the: Root/Quality Chord Symbol __D__   Functional Chord Symbol __I__

i) Circle if the melodic motive at the letters G and H is: (same) or similar or different

j) Add the rests at the letter I.

Bonus - Play this excerpt from the "Hallelujah Chorus" on your instrument.

Ultimate Music Theory Certificate

_____

has successfully completed all the requirements of the

Music Theory Level 5

_____ _____
Music Teacher *Date*

Enriching Lives Through Music Education

www.ingramcontent.com/pod-product-compliance
Lightning Source LLC
Chambersburg PA
CBHW081730100526
44591CB00016B/2561